CH

Life in Ancient Mesopotamia

Other titles in the *Living History* series include:

Life in Ancient Mesopotamia

Don Nardo

San Diego, CA

© 2014 ReferencePoint Press, Inc.
Printed in the United States

For more information, contact:
ReferencePoint Press, Inc.
PO Box 27779
San Diego, CA 92198
www.ReferencePointPress.com

LIBRARY OF CONGRESS CATALOGING-IN-PUBLICATION DATA

Nardo, Don, 1947-
  Life in Ancient Mesopotamia / by Don Nardo.
    pages cm. -- (Living history series)
  Includes bibliographical references and index.
  ISBN-13: 978-1-60152-572-7 (hardback)
  ISBN-10: 1-60152-572-9 (hardback)
  1. Iraq--History--To 634--Juvenile literature. 2. Sumerians--History--Juvenile literature.
  3. Civilization, Assyro-Babylonian--Juvenile literature. I. Title.
  DS69.5N33 2014
  935--dc23

                                                                      2013017163

Contents

Foreword

History is a complex and multifaceted discipline that embraces many different areas of human activity. Given the expansive possibilities for the study of history, it is significant that since the advent of formal writing in the Ancient Near East over six thousand years ago, the contents of most nonfiction historical literature have been overwhelmingly limited to politics, religion, warfare, and diplomacy.

Beginning in the 1960s, however, the focus of many historical works experienced a substantive change worldwide. This change resulted from the efforts and influence of an ever-increasing number of progressive contemporary historians who were entering the halls of academia. This new breed of academician, soon accompanied by many popular writers, argued for a major revision of the study of history, one in which the past would be presented from the ground up. What this meant was that the needs, wants, and thinking of ordinary people should and would become an integral part of the human record. As British historian Mary Fulbrook wrote in her 2005 book, *The People's State: East German Society from Hitler to Honecker,* students should be able to view "history with the people put back in." This approach to understanding the lives and times of people of the past has come to be known as social history. According to contemporary social historians, national and international affairs should be viewed not only from the perspective of those empowered to create policy but also through the eyes of those over whom power is exercised.

The American historian and best-selling author, Louis "Studs" Terkel, was one of the pioneers in the field of social history. He is best remembered for his oral histories, which were firsthand accounts of everyday life drawn from the recollections of interviewees who lived during pivotal events or periods in history. Terkel's first book, *Division Street America* (published in 1967), focuses on urban living in and around Chicago and is a compilation of seventy interviews of immigrants and native-born Americans. It was followed by several other oral histories including *Hard Times* (the 1930s depression), *Working* (people's feelings about their jobs), and his 1985 Pulitzer Prize–winning *The Good War* (about life in America before, during, and after World War II).

In keeping with contemporary efforts to present history by people and about people, ReferencePoint's *Living History* series offers students a journey through recorded history as recounted by those who lived it. While modern sources such as those found in *The Good War* and on radio and TV interviews are readily available, those dating to earlier periods in history are scarcer and often more obscure the further back in time one investigates. These important primary sources are there nonetheless waiting to be discovered in literary formats such as posters, letters, and diaries, and in artifacts such as vases, coins, and tombstones. And they are also found in places as varied as ancient Mesopotamia, Charles Dickens's England, and Nazi concentration camps. The *Living History* series uncovers these and other available sources as they relate the "living history" of real people to their student readers.

Important Events of

BC ca. 9000
Agriculture begins in the Fertile Crescent, the well-watered region stretching across Mesopotamia's northern rim.

ca. 3500–3000
The Sumerians oversee widespread application of the wheel, build the first wagons, and erect the first true cities.

ca. 5000–3500
The Ubaidians, the direct predecessors of the Sumerians, establish numerous villages in Mesopotamia.

ca. 3000
The earliest known medical text is written in the Sumerian city of Nippur.

BC 6000   5000   4000   3000   2000

ca. 5500
The first waves of settlers from the Fertile Crescent move into the Tigris-Euphrates river valley.

ca. 3100
The world's first writing system appears in some of the Sumerian cities.

ca. 2340–2200
The approximate dates for the rise and fall of the first empire, founded by the Akkadian king Sargon the Great.

Ancient Mesopotamia

AD ca. 650
Islamic Arab armies conquer Mesopotamia, then ruled by Persians, ending its ancient era.

1792–1750
Years of the reign of the Babylonian king Hammurabi, author of the region's most famous law code.

721–705
Years of the rule of Assyria's King Sargon II, who orders the building of the region's first underground aqueduct.

1872
The first English translation of the Gilgamesh epic is published.

| 2000 | 1000 | 0 | AD 1000 | 2000 |

668–627
Reign of the former scribe Ashurbanipal, who creates Mesopotamia's most extensive library.

1902
A team of French archaeologists finds a tablet bearing the renowned law code of the Babylonian king Hammurabi.

1646–1626
Babylonian king Ammi-saduqa's reign, in which astronomers collect observations of the planets that have aided modern historians in dating Mesopotamian events.

1775–1761
Reign of Zimri-Lim, king of Mari, who compiles one of the largest literary archives in the region.

Introduction

Lives Dependent on the Rivers

It was no coincidence that the world's earliest major civilizations grew up along the banks of large rivers. Indeed, modern historians identify four chief so-called cradles of human culture, each of which took root in the well-watered soils near the banks of one or more mighty rivers. In China, for example, the powerful Yellow River provided the basis for a flourishing culture. Also, the Nile in northeastern Africa supported the ancient Egyptian civilization, which produced the famous great pyramids. Meanwhile, in India hundreds of cities belonging to the Harappan culture arose along the banks of the Indus River.

Finally, in ancient Mesopotamia, what is now Iraq, the vital waterways were the Tigris and Euphrates Rivers. The culture that appeared in the huge Tigris-Euphrates valley more than six thousand years ago was more than just one of the four great ancient river civilizations. It was also the first of them to spring into existence. Farms and villages appeared in the valley as early as seventy-five hundred years ago.

Like the Chinese, Egyptians, and Harappans, the inhabitants of Mesopotamia relied on the local rivers for life-giving water. In fact, this is what had first attracted early humans to the Tigris-Euphrates area. Small clans of primitive hunter-gatherers, who followed herds of antelope and other creatures they killed for food, stopped at the riverbanks to drink. They saw that their prey was also drawn to these waterways for the same reason. So before moving on, the clans took advantage of the good hunting and stocked up on meat and hides.

Life in the Fertile Crescent

Later in ancient times the Tigris and Euphrates drew people to their banks for a different and ultimately more historic reason. Lying several miles west and north of the Mesopotamian river plains stretched a sweeping semicircle-shaped region. It included large sectors of what are now Syria, southern Turkey, and northern Iraq. Like parts of Mesopotamia, it had plentiful rains and extremely rich soil. So modern historians gave the entire region, including much of Mesopotamia, the name Fertile Crescent.

It was in the northern reaches of this area that agriculture first began circa 9000 BC, or about eleven thousand years ago. The residents figured out how to grow wheat, barley, lentils, cucumbers, lettuce, grapes, and other crops. They also raised and bred cattle, sheep, goats, pigs, and other livestock. Together, those crops and animals composed such an ample and dependable food source that the people of the Fertile Crescent abandoned the hunter-gatherer lifestyle. They settled down and built small villages beside their farms. Each of these tiny communities featured a few dozen huts made from thatch and other natural materials.

The new agricultural lifestyle proved so successful that the little villages of the northern sector of the Fertile Crescent steadily increased in number and size. In turn, this population boom inspired the more restless members of society to move southward onto the plains of the great rivers. In about 5500 BC they became the first of several waves of settlers who stayed permanently in the Tigris-Euphrates valley.

> **WORDS IN CONTEXT**
> **thatch**
> Bundled tree branches.

A Blank Agricultural Slate

These immigrants discovered that they could now practice agriculture on a much larger scale than they could in their original homelands to the west and north. As ancient Near East scholar Gwendolyn Leick explains, they found that the soil along the riverbanks "was fertile enough to guarantee abundant and multiple crops." In addition, they noticed that the highly fruitful earth in the area had extremely few rocks. This made it "relatively easy to dig," Leick points out,

> which allowed for the construction of canals and subsidiary waterways. Thus, the alluvial plains became a *tabula rasa* [blank slate] to be cultivated and populated at will. Villages and cities grew up along the rivers, as well as between them, following the course of man-made or natural side-arms and canals which assured a year-round supply of water and provided the main means of communication.[1]

In this way, little by little a large-scale civilization—the world's first—grew up along the two Mesopotamian rivers. The people became dependent on those water sources. At the same time, the rivers provided the means for the growth of a progressively more complex society. In the words of the late American historian W.H. McNeill, the "riches of the river valley gave rise to a comparatively dense population [and the] diverging interests and outlook of fishers, herdsmen, and cultivators, all of whom had to live cheek and jowl with one another."[2]

WORDS IN CONTEXT
alluvial
Laid down a little at a time by flowing water.

In turn, this situation stimulated the creation of larger social units. "It became possible," McNeill writes,

> for relatively dense populations to sustain life in the river valleys of Mesopotamia. And the presence of such large populations in turn provided the mass labor power needed for erecting monumental [large-scale] structures, for extending the system of dikes and canals to new ground year by year, and for performing the tasks of long-distance transport required by the growing complexity of their style of life.[3]

Thus, from its crude beginnings in a distant bygone age, Mesopotamian civilization was through-and-through a river culture. The people's daily needs, including drinking, bathing, and irrigating crops, relied on the great rivers. Moreover, the rivers dictated the kinds of foods they con-

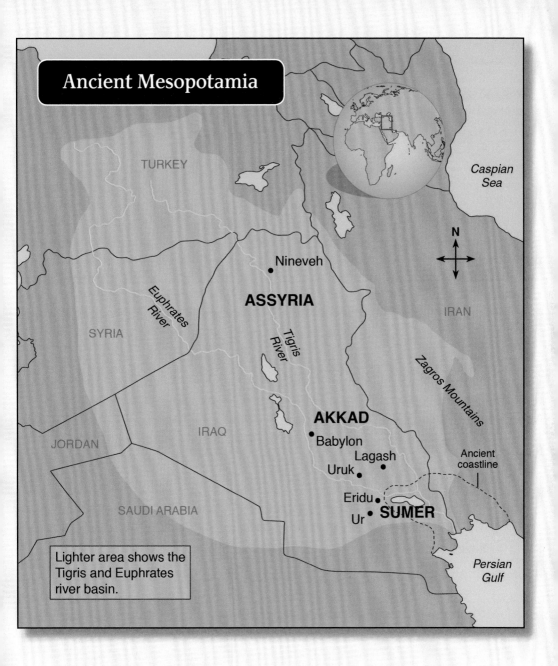

Ancient Mesopotamia

TURKEY

Caspian
Sea

Nineveh

ASSYRIA

Euphrates
River

Tigris
River

IRAN

SYRIA

Zagros Mountains

AKKAD

Babylon

Lagash

IRAQ

JORDAN

Ancient
coastline

Uruk

Eridu

SAUDI ARABIA

Ur • **SUMER**

N

Lighter area shows the
Tigris and Euphrates
river basin.

Persian
Gulf

sumed, the types of building materials they used to erect their houses and cities, the kinds of professions they held, the nature of their myths, and many more critical aspects of their lives. So interconnected were they with the *Idiglat* and the *Buranun*—their names for the Tigris and Euphrates— that outsiders automatically associated them with those rivers. Indeed, the chief term that posterity came to use for the region, *Mesopotamia*, is Greek for "the land between the rivers."

Chapter One

City-States and Their Residents

When the first waves of settlers migrated into the Tigris-Euphrates river valley around 5500 BC, they built small villages like those they had left behind in the northern parts of the Fertile Crescent. Over time some of these hamlets slowly grew into towns with populations of one thousand people or more. Among those in northern Mesopotamia were Tepe Gawra and Choga Mami. The new towns in the south, near the Persian Gulf, included Ur, Uruk, and Tell al-Ubaid.

Modern historians refer to the people who lived in these small communities as Ubaidians, after Tell al-Ubaid. (What they called themselves remains a mystery.) Accordingly, scholars call the phase of Mesopotamian history lasting from about 5000 to 3500 BC the Ubaidian period.

A typical Ubaidian village or small town was made up of a cluster of huts constructed of hard-packed earth and/or reeds gathered from the rivers. As time went on people added other, larger structures. Among them were granaries—essentially big storage sheds for grain. These early Mesopotamian farmers learned the importance of storing extra grain in years of good harvests to feed the populace during years when harvests were not so good. Some towns also started to feature a central earthen mound with a one-room building on its summit. Historians think these were the first crude versions of religious temples.

Emergence of the First City

Little is known about the Ubaidians' customs or social organization. What is certain is that they kept their communities small and never took the major step of expanding them into true cities. That fateful stride was taken by a new large-scale population group that assumed control of the region in the mid-3000s BC. Early modern historians called them the Sumerians, a term derived from the word *Sumer*, which later ancient residents of the area used to describe southern Mesopotamia. *Kengir* was the name the Sumerians themselves gave the area. It meant "civilized land."

This turned out to be an extremely fitting choice of words because the Sumerians proceeded to create the world's first cities. Never before had anyone dwelled in an urban setting and been subject to its abundance of both benefits and drawbacks. "A new style of human life had emerged," W.H. McNeill remarks. It was "characterized by a complexity, wealth, and general impressiveness that justify the epithet [name] 'civilized.'"[4]

A reference to the very first city, Eridu, figured prominently in one of the chief Mesopotamian creation stories. In the beginning, it says, "All the lands were sea." In other words, there were no dry lands. But then the great god Marduk "created dirt," so he could "settle the gods in the dwelling of their hearts' delight," that is, a temple. The problem was where to put a temple, much less any other structure. "A house had not been made," the creation story continues. "A city had not been built." As if this lack of cities was particularly crucial, the sacred narrative repeated it, saying, "A city had not been made!"[5]

> **WORDS IN CONTEXT**
> **granaries**
> Large storage sheds for grain.

To solve this problem, in a magnificent feat of engineering the marvelous Marduk erected the first city. "Then Eridu was made," the story goes on, and the holy temple compound, the Esagila, was built. Then the gods happily cried out in unison, solemnly calling it "the holy city, the dwelling of their hearts' delight."[6]

Small Independent Nations

Eridu and the other early Sumerian cities were many times larger and more complex than anything the Ubaidians had built. Each Sumerian urban center featured thousands of houses and tens of thousands of people. It also had shops for merchants, palaces for rulers, and large religious temples like the Esagila, all surrounded by high defensive walls that were often dozens of miles in circumference.

Thus, thanks to the Sumerians, the agricultural revolution had led directly to an urban revolution. In the latter, new engineering concepts combined with the efficient organization of thousands of workers to produce monumental architectural achievements. "Cities arose," historian Stephen Bertman writes, "that guarded their wealth behind moats and gated walls, while within these walls—amid winding streets and huddled dwellings and shops—stood administrative centers and temples, the new institutions of an invention called civilization."[7]

The idea of the city was so popular in early Mesopotamia that it came to dominate both the physical and political landscapes. "By the end of the third millennium BC," or about 2000 BC, Gwendolyn Leick points out, "90 percent of the population in southern Mesopotamia was living in cities."[8] It is important to emphasize that these cities, among them Ur (now dozens of times larger than it had been in Ubaidian times), Kish, Lagash, Umma, Sippar, and Nippur, were not dependent elements of a larger Sumerian nation. Instead, they were independent city-states, each of which saw itself as a small but sovereign nation.

Farmers, Crops, and Livestock

Such a city-state included not only the walled urban center but also the numerous villages, farms, and irrigation canals surrounding it. The many residents of the urban center required a great deal of food on a daily, monthly, and yearly basis. The local farmers were expected to supply most of that food, although some was also imported via trade with other city-states.

The farmers and their families and slaves, who made up a minority of the state's population, were its only residents who spent most of their time outside the urban center's lofty walls. Most of these rural folk lived in small thatch and mud-brick huts, many of them grouped into tiny villages. They walked or rode donkey-pulled wagons to the fields early in the morning. Hours later, when the sun dipped toward the horizon and shadows began to lengthen, they walked or rode home.

The leading crop these farmers grew was barley, a kind of wheat used to make a type of flatbread that is still eaten in Iraq today. Other dietary staples that came from barley were a thick porridge eaten for breakfast and a very nutritious and flavorsome beer. Sumerian and other Mesopotamian farmers also grew beans, lentils, peas, cucumbers, lettuce, garlic, figs, and grapes.

Because the temperature often rose to more than 100°F (38°C) in the daytime, the farmers had to find a way to shade these crops from the hot sun. So they developed a method called "shade-tree gardening." It consisted of planting the crops beneath the broad branches of palm and other fruit trees. Usually, planting occurred in the fall or early winter, and the foodstuffs were harvested in April or May.

The plow the farmers used to plant those crops was fashioned from wood and pulled by oxen. In Ubaidian and Sumerian times (before 2000

As with the cities of ancient Sumeria, high defensive walls surround the palace and temple of ancient Babylon. As depicted in a modern illustration, merchants and townspeople conduct business within the walled city as well as on its outskirts.

In Their Own Words

Tips for Farmers

In the 1920s at Ur, noted archaeologist Charles Leonard Woolley found fragments of a farmer's almanac dating to circa 1700 BC. After the fragments were pieced together, another leading scholar, Samuel N. Kramer, translated the document, which is excerpted here.

> When you are about to take hold of your field for cultivation, keep a sharp eye on the opening of the dikes, ditches, and mounds so that when you flood the field the water will not rise too high in it. When you have emptied it of water, watch the field's water-soaked ground that it stays virile [fertile] ground for you. Let shod oxen, that is, oxen whose hooves are protected in one way or another, trample it for you; and after having its weeds ripped out by them, and the field made level ground, dress it evenly with narrow axes weighing no more than two-thirds of a pound each. Following which let the pickax wielder eradicate the ox hooves for you and smooth them out. . . . When you are about to plow your field, keep your eye on the man who puts in the barley seed. Let him drop the grain uniformly two fingers deep, and use up one shekel of barley for each *garush* [about 27 square yards, or 22 sq. m]. If the barley seed does not sink in properly, change your [plow]share, the "tongue of the plow." If the [fragment missing], then plow diagonal furrows where you have plowed straight furrows.

Quoted in Samuel N. Kramer, *The Sumerians: Their History, Culture, and Character*. Chicago: University of Chicago Press, 1971, pp. 340–42.

BC), it was common for an assistant to walk behind the plowman and fling the seeds into the furrows the plow had just dug out. Sometime in the second millennium BC, however, a new kind of plow came into use. Mounted on it was a funnel, which one filled with seeds. As the farmer guided the oxen along and the plow dug a furrow, a few seeds trickled down from the funnel into that groove.

The oxen employed in planting were not the only animals raised in the countryside surrounding the urban centers. Sheep and goats were bred by the thousands. The sheep were valuable both as a food source and for their fleeces, from which people spun yarn to make various kinds of clothes.

The flocks of sheep were often tended by teenagers and even younger children. This allowed the adults in a farming family to devote their time to more arduous tasks. It was common to move the flocks from pasture to pasture as the growing season progressed. In contrast, other domesticated animals, including cattle, pigs, donkeys, ducks, and geese, were generally kept in the same area year-round. Some of the animals raised in a typical city-state were bred (and some crops were grown) on large farming estates run by the religious temples and royal palaces.

Urban Center Layout

The temples and palaces themselves stood well protected inside the urban center's walls. Archaeologists think that most such centers in ancient Mesopotamia were laid out more or less as Uruk was. Today its ruins lie beside the village of Tell al-Warka in southern Iraq. (*Warka* is the Arabic version of *Uruk*, which is also the basis for the modern country name *Iraq*.)

When excavators unearthed those ruins in the early twentieth century, they confirmed what a surviving ancient writing from the region had claimed. Namely, roughly a third of the urban center was devoted to temples and their holy grounds. Another third of the center contained open areas owned and run by the palace, that is, the government—essentially a group of officials appointed by the king who dwelled in that palace. The remaining third featured private houses along with a few shops and workrooms (the ancient equivalent of factories). In those shops and workrooms, artisans, or craftspeople, produced pottery and other hand-made items.

The more recent excavation of the urban center at Mashkan-shapir, a few miles southeast of Uruk, revealed a similar layout. The residential

A farmer plows the rocky desert landscape of Iraq in much the same fashion as farmers who lived there thousands of years ago. Early plows dropped seeds through a funnel into grooves dug into the soil.

areas of Mashkan-shapir, Yale University scholar Karen R. Nemet-Nejat explains, were made up of

> a network of streets, and most homes were entered through narrow alleyways and culs-de-sacs. The layout of the narrow streets was like a maze. The street surfaces were uneven, in part due to the constant rebuilding of homes on previous foundations that were never leveled, and in part because garbage was dumped into the streets. Dogs and other scavenging animals ate some rubbish, but the rest was dried by the sun and walked on. At Mashkan-shapir, all residential areas included [workrooms for] artisans.[9]

Free Workers and Their Occupations

The people who lived and worked in these residential sectors of the cities were mostly members of the lower social classes, who made up the vast majority of the city-state's populace. Those underclasses included freemen, or free persons, of modest means; serfs; and slaves. (In ancient Mesopotamia, a serf was someone whose social status lay somewhere between that of a freeman and a slave.)

Among the freemen in a city-state were farmers and others who lived and worked in the countryside. Some owned their own small plots of land, while others hired themselves out as helpers on the big estates owned by the temples and nobles. The rest of the community's free workers were craftspeople and laborers who lived and worked in the urban center. According to Bertman, they had a wide range of occupations, including

> WORDS IN CONTEXT
> **artisan**
> A skilled craftsperson or other worker.

> brickmakers, stone masons, and carpenters, as well as decorative artists such as sculptors and painters. The food trades were practiced by such workers as fishermen, butchers, bakers, and brewers. Meanwhile, consumer goods were manufactured by bronze

workers, silversmiths, goldsmiths, glassmakers, potters (the most common craft), leather workers and shoemakers, [cloth] weavers, reed [weavers], and basket makers, jewelers, and seal-stone cutters. Transportation needs were met by wagon makers, wagon drivers, shipwrights, and boatmen. In addition, there were street vendors, shopowners, and innkeepers, as well as prostitutes.[10]

These workers had no universities or other formal schools in which to learn their trades. Instead, in a time-honored tradition stretching back into the dim reaches of prehistory, they passed on knowledge of their crafts to the next generation via the apprentice system. If an apprentice worked diligently and demonstrated mastery of certain skills, he became a journeyman, or capable, proficient worker. Over time he might even become a master, a widely respected expert in his craft with his own young apprentices.

A master and his apprentices typically developed a close relationship. In many cases the apprentices lived in the master's home for a number of years and looked upon him as a father figure. As a result, laws evolved to protect the rights of both the master and the apprentices' real parents.

One such law is part of the major legal code compiled by the renowned Babylonian ruler Hammurabi, who reigned circa 1792 to 1750 BC. It says that when a master "has undertaken to rear a child and teaches him his craft," the apprentice "cannot be demanded back"[11] by the apprentice's parents. Thus, the apprentice was in a sense the master's foster or adopted child for as long as the master was teaching him the trade.

Masters and apprentices were not the only workers who developed close relationships. Archaeologists have found evidence that most or all of the workers who had a particular occupation came together to form a guild. That organization was not like modern labor unions that stage strikes in hopes of obtaining pay raises. Ancient Mesopotamian craft guilds were essentially fellowships whose members shared specific skills and life experiences. They often developed friendships, worshipped together, and attended one another's wedding parties and funerals.

Looking Back

Mazes of Houses

Popular historian Michael Wood here describes the look and feel of the various divisions of an ancient Sumerian city-state.

A big city-state like Lagash had 36,000 male adults, Uruk perhaps the same. They were closely organized and controlled. In Nippur at a later period, there were 200 subsidiary villages in its territory, clustered around five main canals and sixty lesser ones, joined by a web of countless small irrigation ditches, all of which were subject to rules, duties and control, a constant source of [legal disputes]. As for the physical make-up of the city itself, according to the [Sumerian epic poem the] *Epic of Gilgamesh*, Uruk was one-third built up [with homes and shops], one-third gardens, one-third temple property. Excavated streets in Ur and Nippur look just like the warrens [mazes] of houses still visible in [the region]. The design of houses in the ancient cities was identical to that used up till the advent of air conditioning, with central courtyards, windcatchers, and serdabs (sunken rooms) to keep the ferocious summer heat at bay.

Michael Wood, *Legacy: The Search for Ancient Cultures*. New York: Sterling, 1992, p. 27.

Slaves and Serfs

The other members of the lower classes, slaves and serfs, usually possessed fewer skills than freemen and therefore performed mostly menial jobs and tasks. Slaves, who came to be called *wardu* (technically male slaves) in Mesopotamia, fell into servitude in various ways. At first, most were foreigners captured in military campaigns. Thereafter, they worked on state-sponsored building projects, including digging canals and hauling the stones used in the construction of defensive walls, palaces, and temples. Over time these "public" slaves came to do the most difficult or boring kinds of labor on the large temple estates.

WORDS IN CONTEXT

wardu

The most common Akkadian word for slaves.

There were also private slaves owned by individual families and households. The number of slaves per home is uncertain, in part because it varied considerably according to region, era, and family income. But modern experts estimate an overall average of one, two, or three slaves in households of modest means and thirty, forty, or more slaves in wealthy households.

Private slaves most often cleaned the house, ran errands, and/or helped with cooking and child rearing. A few of the more trustworthy slaves aided their masters as shop clerks or personal assistants. Also, male and female household slaves sometimes formed relationships and had children together. This created another avenue to the slavery institution—being born into it.

Still another way that people became slaves was when freemen voluntarily, though reluctantly, did so—a custom known as debt-slavery. Typically, such a person owed a creditor a lot of money and had no other way to repay it. So he sold himself, his children, or even the whole family to the creditor. The slave or slaves continued to labor for the creditor for a set number of years until they finally earned their freedom. The terms and periods of such deals are briefly stated in one of Hammurabi's laws: "If any one fail to meet a claim for debt, and sell himself, his wife, his son, and daughter for money or give them away to forced labor, they shall work for three years in the house of the man who bought them, or the proprietor, and in the fourth year they shall be set free."[12]

Mesopotamian laws also provided for how slaves could be treated or punished. For example, penalties for runaway slaves included beating them or starving them for several days. Killing a slave was extremely rare, mainly because he or she was a valuable piece of property that could be expensive to replace. In any case very few slaves tried to escape. The reason was that everyone, including slaves, saw slavery as a perfectly natural and inevitable condition that even the gods sanctioned. As a result, the vast majority of people had no sympathy for an escaped slave and refused to help him or her. Moreover, anyone who did aid a runaway faced the death penalty.

Unlike slaves, Mesopotamian serfs could not be bought and sold like property. So technically, serfs were free. However, as historian H.W.F. Saggs puts it, "often their economic circumstances were no better than those of slaves."[13] As was the case later in medieval Europe, serfs in the ancient Tigris-Euphrates region were mainly poor agricultural workers. They were so poor, in fact, that they were totally dependent on whoever owned the land on which they toiled. So, although a serf was legally allowed to quit work and move somewhere else, more often than not he

A terra-cotta relief from ancient Mesopotamia shows a woman weaving. Mesopotamian cities provided work for skilled craftspeople and laborers in many occupations—among them silversmiths, shoemakers, jewelers, butchers, and weavers.

lacked even the small amount of money needed to travel and look for work. There was no choice, therefore, but to stay in the same situation for the rest of his life.

The Upper Social Classes

Well above the serfs, slaves, and freemen on the social ladder was a small but dominant group of upper-class individuals, headed by the most powerful of them all—the reigning king. Mesopotamian monarchs derived their absolute authority in part from their lineage. That is, they were members of the royal family, which in most cases was part of a family line of rulers, or dynasty, going back several generations.

These kings claimed that their supreme authority also came from a special connection between themselves and one or more gods. This is shown in the region's ancient writings, which mention that certain rulers were chosen or guided by heavenly deities. There are references to a monarch being the son of a god and to kings displaying a radiant aura, or halo-like light, around their bodies. Also, in ancient Mesopotamian art, kings were frequently shown standing beside various deities as if socializing with them.

> **WORDS IN CONTEXT**
> **dynasty**
> A line of rulers who are all members of a single family.

Because of this supposed extraordinary relationship with the divine, national rulers enjoyed numerous special powers and privileges. The king was the highest priest in his nation-state, for example. He was also the supreme commander of the army and had the power to appoint governors and other administrators. In addition, he received and entertained high officials and foreign ambassadors, had the last word in legal disputes and matters of justice, and enjoyed the finest foods along with the constant attention of hundreds of servants and guards.

Directly below the king on the social ladder, but still comfortably above freemen, were the community's nobles. Relatively few in number, these well-to-do, privileged individuals included members of the priesthood, high military officers, royal advisers and administrators, and governors of other cities, if any, controlled by the local monarch. They dwelled in comfortable homes, had servants to tend to their needs, and often owned farming estates consisting of many acres.

The Torch of Civilization Passes

Whether one calls them city-states, city-nations, or simply cities, the unique Mesopotamian political units that these kings and nobles oversaw were a Sumerian invention. Mostly self-sufficient and economically successful, each was intensely proud of its local traditions and customs. Furthermore, it fiercely defended its traditions and economic assets against any aggressors, of which there was usually no shortage.

In fact, as the third millennium BC wore on, it became fairly common for one city to attempt to take over a neighboring city's canals, farmlands, and villages. This naturally led to battles and wars for dominance, and the balance of power in the region was always shifting back and forth. At one point, for instance, both Uruk and Ur defeated Kish, which lost much influence and respect. But not long afterward Kish rebounded, struck back, and regained most of its lost territory.

Fortunately for all involved, these conflicts long remained small-scale, most often pitting only one city against another. Moreover, the contests were decided mainly in formal battles fought on the open plains lying between the cities. The urban centers and their populations remained largely untouched and intact.

But just as the Sumerians had pioneered both the city and wars among cities, they eventually introduced still another fateful historical milestone. In the early 2300s BC, Sargon, an ambitious young man from northern Mesopotamia, conquered all of the Sumerian cities, thereby creating the world's first empire. One of his surviving inscriptions reads: "The city Uruk he subjugated and its wall he tore down. In the battle with the inhabitants of Uruk he was victorious. Lugalzaggisi, king of Uruk he captured in the battle." Later, the document says, Sargon "was victorious in the battle with the inhabitants of Ur," and later still, all the "territory from Lagash to the sea he subjugated."[14]

Over time, like all empires do sooner or later, Sargon's fell apart, and the Sumerian cities reasserted themselves. However, by about 2000 BC these states had seriously declined in power and influence. Thereafter, stronger groups and dynasties, whose members spoke non-Sumerian languages, took power in the region. The millennium that followed witnessed the torch of civilization in Mesopotamia pass from the Sumerians to others, at first especially to Akkadian-speaking peoples. Some dwelled in the great river valley's northern plains—an area that became known as Assyria. Others flourished in the south, closer to the Persian Gulf, a region that came to be called Babylonia.

The Babylonians and Assyrians did not replace Sumerian customs, beliefs, and lifestyles but rather absorbed them. "From their Sumerian predecessors," the late historian Samuel N. Kramer explains, they adopted "much of their religion, literature, law, and art,"[15] thereby preserving them. As had been true in the past, continuity and respect for tradition remained paramount in the area. So social and other change occurred at a proverbial snail's pace. The result was a situation that people in today's rapidly changing world find extremely odd. Everyday life and customs for a Sumerian in 2700 BC were destined to be little different than those for a Babylonian or Assyrian a thousand or more years later.

Chapter Two

Home, Family, and Children

Daily life in ancient Sumerian, Babylonian, and Assyrian cities revolved around two separate but intimately connected spheres. One was the home, the private domain of the culture's most basic and in many ways most important social unit—the family. The other social sphere was the local community, or the city-state itself. The community was in a very real sense a large collection of individual families that worked together for the greater good of all involved.

Mesopotamian tradition and custom viewed the family as a sort of tool with which people could and should make the community stronger and more stable. In general, family life was equated with, or made possible by, marriage. In turn, marriage was intended more as a way to prop up and perpetuate society than as an expression of love between spouses, as it is today. "Marriage," Stephen Bertman writes, "was fundamentally a business arrangement designed to assure and perpetuate an orderly society. Though there was an inevitable emotional component to marriage, its prime intent in the eyes of the state was not companionship, but procreation [having children]; not personal happiness in the present, but communal continuity for the future."[16]

Construction Materials

Homes and urban centers provided security and sanctuary for Mesopotamian life's two primary spheres—the community and family. For the community, the urban center with its high defensive walls was the enclosed sanctuary, or safe zone. For the family, the sanctuary was the individual house. Here, the word *house* is used in the modern sense—as a single small building in which one family dwelled. In ancient Mesopotamia, by contrast, the word for "house," *bitum*, had numerous meanings. It could refer not only to a building but also to a family, large or small; to a temple estate or palace household, including hundreds of slaves; and even to a business that produced pottery or other items in a large workroom. Ancient texts, Gwendolyn Leick points out, "do not differentiate between types of household into, say, private and public households, urban and non-urban, or large and small."[17]

Most urban homes, or townhouses, in cities like Ur and Babylon were fairly similar in construction and appearance, although their size could vary. Typically, they were built of mud-bricks— mud or clay bricks formed in standardized wooden molds and left out in the sun to dry. The main advantages of using these bricks were, first, that the materials were plentiful in the river valley. Stone and timber were scarce and had to be imported at considerable expense. Second, mud-bricks were extremely easy to make and use.

One obvious disadvantage of building with mud-bricks was that they cracked and disintegrated rapidly, especially during storms. Also, it took little effort to break or tunnel through them, which was pretty much an invitation to thieves. To help alleviate these drawbacks, where possible or affordable, builders made brick walls several feet thick. This had the added benefit of making a house's interior better insulated from the hot sun so common in the region. Another way to keep interior spaces cooler was to whitewash the outer walls, which reflected away a portion of the sunlight.

House Layouts and Rooms

The size of townhouses varied, mainly according to the owners' financial means. Excavations carried out in the ruins of ancient cities throughout the region show that most homes—those of families of average yearly incomes—measured about 8 by 18 feet (2.4 by 5.4 m). These relatively small structures featured two, three, or four rooms.

The houses of successful merchants, government officials, and other wealthy individuals were fewer in number but a good deal larger than average dwellings. Well-to-do homes usually had several rooms, divided between two stories. In Uruk, Nippur, Babylon, and other cities, such structures featured a layout similar to many modern homes in the region. There was a central courtyard, open to the sky, with a number of rooms arranged along the courtyard's four sides. The kitchen was almost always on the ground floor. It had a large brick hearth used for both cooking and providing some extra warmth in cooler evenings.

The ruins of the ancient Sumerian city of Uruk illustrate the temporary nature of mud-brick homes and other buildings. Although the clay needed for the bricks was plentiful and easy to use, mud-brick buildings could not withstand storms or the march of time.

In Their Own Words

When a Free Woman Married a Slave

It was widely common in ancient Mesopotamia for slaves to dwell in the same houses as their masters, and some slaves even had children with their masters. It was therefore necessary to have laws covering the legal status and economic rights of all involved. One of the laws introduced by the Babylonian king Hammurabi, reproduced below, protected the inheritance of a free-born woman who married a slave (if and after the slave died).

[If] a State slave or the slave of a freedman marry a man's [free-born] daughter, and after he marries her she bring a dowry from [her] father's house, if then they both enjoy it and found a household, and accumulate means, if then the slave die, then she who was free born may take her dowry, and all that her husband and she had earned. She shall divide them into two parts, one-half the master for the slave shall take, and the other half shall the free-born woman take for her children. If the free-born woman had no gift [dowry], she shall take all that her husband and she had earned and divide it into two parts. And the master of the slave shall take one-half and she shall take the other for her children.

Quoted in L.W. King, trans., "Hammurabi's Code of Laws," Exploring Ancient World Culture, University of Evansville. http://eawc.evansville.edu.

Most Mesopotamian houses lacked modern-style bathrooms. A person usually relieved him- or herself into a pottery jar. Every day or two, a slave or family member emptied the jar into a pit maintained by the state on the outer edge of the urban center. Most bathing took place in the nearest river or canal. Only the wealthiest homes featured inside bathrooms. In such cases the toilets were round holes cut into wooden benches. The wastes fell down into buckets, to be emptied later or passed through baked clay channels to cesspools situated underground beside the house. In Babylonia in the first millennium BC, the palaces had set-ups for showers, although the water was not piped in. Instead, the king or a member of his family stood or sat in the center of a small, brick-lined chamber and allowed servants to gently pour containers of water over him or her.

Furniture, Clothing, and Personal Accessories

A variety of evidence (including ancient writings and artistic renderings, along with a few actual surviving items) provides a fairly clear idea of the furniture in Mesopotamian townhouses. Average homes featured chairs and stools fashioned from palm wood and/or woven reeds. People ate their meals off of low wooden tables quite similar to modern versions in the region. In contrast, there were no modern-style closets, so people stored their clothes and other belongings in reed baskets or chests made of palm wood or baked clay.

Beds like those used today did exist in houses in Babylon and other Mesopotamian cities, but only well-to-do people could afford to own them. According to Karen R. Nemet-Nejat,

> Beds were usually made of a frame and supporting base of wood, though sometimes rope, interwoven reeds, or crisscrosses of metal strips were used. The bed provided support for mattresses stuffed with wool, goat's hair, or palm fiber. Bedding included linen sheets, mattresses, cushions, and blankets. Medical texts often mentioned patients who "took to their bed." Of course, not everyone owned a bed. The poor slept on straw or reed mats.[18]

Archaeological evidence also shows how the ancient inhabitants of the Tigris-Euphrates valley dressed. In the third millennium BC, the heyday of the Sumerians, the most common fabric employed for clothing was sheep's wool. Men most often went bare-chested and wore a long skirt-like garment that hung from waist to ankles. Women wore a toga-like outfit draped over one shoulder. For accessories like hats and shoes, people used felt, a material made from crushed sheep's hair. (Cotton and silk were not introduced into the region until many centuries later.)

In the late 2000s BC, men gave up the bare-chested look and donned long robes that draped over one shoulder. Women's garments still covered most of the body but now draped over both shoulders and featured a plunging open V-neck in the front. These clothing styles continued to be popular for many centuries.

Those who could afford it often added various accessories to their outfits. These included such items as men's trousers, caps, and walking sticks, women's hair ribbons, and outer cloaks and jewelry worn by both genders. The jewelry was fashioned from gold, silver, copper, lapis lazuli, agate, and colorful handmade beads. In addition, upper-class women and a few men as well wore makeup, including lip color and eyeliner. Modern excavators of the royal cemetery at Ur discovered some women's makeup kits that contained tiny traces of yellow, green, blue, and black eyeliner. Other common personal accessories included combs made of wood and ivory, hand mirrors of polished bronze and silver, and metal tweezers not unlike those people use today.

> **WORDS IN CONTEXT**
> **lapis lazuli**
> A semiprecious stone having an intense blue color.

Common Foods

Archaeologists have also found evidence revealing much about what the residents of ancient Mesopotamia ate. People of average income or less consumed mainly grains, vegetables, and fruits, supplemented by fish from time to time. From the grains—among them barley, rye, and emmer wheat—they made porridge and flat, unleavened breads. It was

Looking Back

Assyrian Women's Submissive Position

The Akkadian-speaking Assyrians, who dwelled in northern Mesopotamia, are often noted for their warlike attributes. Although it is true that military matters played a major role in their society, a large portion of their energies were devoted to maintaining well-ordered, if strict, family and social lives. Scholar Norman B. Hunt here summarizes the subservient position of Assyrian women in the home.

Assyrian society was decidedly patriarchal. Women were under the jurisdiction and authority of a male head of family [usually their fathers], and later came under that of the father-in-law into whose house they moved following a marriage arranged by the male members of the two families. They had few property rights. Even jewelry given to the bride as a marriage gift was the property of her husband. Girls could be legally married at ten years of age, although marriage contracts from the period [the late second millennium BC] suggest the average was sixteen, which, incidentally, was also the age at which a boy became eligible for military service. Marriage was usually monogamous, but this refers to legal status. It was not uncommon for men to have concubines [live-in mistresses] and to use prostitutes.

Norman B. Hunt, *Historical Atlas of Ancient Mesopotamia*. New York: Facts On File, 2004, pp. 94–95.

common practice among members of all social classes to mix milk, fish oil, sesame seed oil, or even fruit juice into the dough, making it thicker and more nutritious.

The most popular vegetables throughout society were onions and garlic, which appeared in a large number of recipes. Cabbage, carrots, radishes, beets, peas, and lentils were also widely eaten, as were fruits such as dates, apples, cherries, apricots, plums, and figs. People in the region did not raise bees, so honey was not readily available. It could be imported from Egypt and elsewhere, but only rich people could afford it. So more easily obtainable date juice was the most frequently used food sweetener in Mesopotamia.

Members of the lower classes ate meat mainly as a luxury during religious holidays, whereas well-to-do people were able to afford meat on a weekly or even daily basis. The meat of lambs, pigs, gazelle, deer, and geese and other birds were widely popular. The custom was to eat these creatures soon after they were slaughtered because, with no way to keep them cold, they spoiled quickly in the region's hot weather. At least some meat was preserved for modest periods by salting it or drying it in the sun.

Women's Rights, Duties, and Jobs

The specific array of foods an individual family regularly ate depended on what was available seasonally, what sorts of foods the father or other head of household could afford, and to some degree what he personally preferred. This was because most Mesopotamian families were patriarchal, or run by the father (*abum* in Akkadian). Also, by law, when the father died the house and other family property passed from him to his son (*marum*) or sons. When the property was split up among two or more offspring, the law made one of several options available. The heirs could trade their land parcels with one another so as to end up with ones that suited them best; they could pool their parcels and divide future profits equally; or one sibling could buy out the others.

> **WORDS IN CONTEXT**
> *abum*
> The word for "father" in ancient Akkadian.

These hair ornaments, earrings, and necklaces—found in a royal burial pit—were probably worn by the women attendants of a queen from the ancient Mesopotamian city of Ur. The pieces are made from gold and feature lapis lazuli and carnelian stones.

The mother (*ummum*) in the family usually had little legal standing in inheritance and most other matters. She was expected to support her husband's decisions and follow his advice. Daughters born into the family were also in a socially and legally subservient position. They had to obey the father until they got married and left his house, after which they had to do the bidding of their husband.

There were a handful of exceptions to this rule of female second-class citizenship. In some of the Sumerian cities, particularly Ur, from where most of the evidence comes, queens, princesses, and high priestesses were accorded higher social status and respect than other women. Excavations of Ur's royal cemetery were revealing. The bodies in several women's graves bore special badges of authority, apparently connected somehow to religious ceremonies. "It appears that at least in ceremonial contexts," Leick says, "certain women were regarded as especially powerful and seem to have derived their elevated rank from professional status rather than from kinship [ties] as daughters or wives of powerful men."[19]

These wealthy, unusually fortunate women had servants to cater to their every whim and desire. So they must be seen as rare exceptions to the rule of women's subservient status. The vast majority of Mesopotamian women had no political rights and few legal ones. Many of them worked on farms, helping their husbands plant, harvest, prune vines, and tow barges upriver. In the urban centers most women were housewives who oversaw the children and servants in homes. Others worked outside the home, some in shops and workrooms, particularly those that produced textiles. Still others were cooks, chambermaids, and barmaids or dancers, singers, and musicians who entertained in taverns.

No matter what they did for a living, as second-class citizens working women automatically earned half of what men made in the same jobs. Also, women got no pay at all while they were menstruating. This was because age-old superstitions held that they could not be productive when having their periods.

Ups and Downs of Marriage

No matter what duties or jobs women performed, the importance society placed on marriage dictated that sooner or later they take husbands and have children. The kind of romantic love idolized in modern Western society may have now and then played a role. In the vast majority of cases, however, marriages were arranged by relatives, most often fathers or grandfathers, and a young woman had no say in choosing a husband. The typical bride was in her teens, whereas her husband-to-be was in his twenties or thirties.

As the wedding date grew near, the groom (or his father or uncle) bargained with the bride's father (or other guardian) about various financial matters. The bride's father agreed to supply the groom with a dowry. It consisted of one or more valuable objects such as furniture, jewelry, slaves, or bars of copper, silver, or other metals. These were intended to help maintain the woman's upkeep in the marriage.

Over time, fairly elaborate laws pertaining to dowries evolved. In Babylonia, for example, a statute enacted by Hammurabi ensured that neither the husband nor the woman's father could profit from the dowry if the woman died after producing male children. "If a man marry a woman," the law stated, "and she bear sons to him, if then this woman die, then shall her father have no claim on her dowry; this belongs to her sons."[20] By contrast, if the woman had not yet produced any sons, the husband profited under certain conditions and the bride's father under others.

As has been true in all places and times, some Mesopotamian marriages did not work out. A woman could divorce her husband if she could prove that he beat or otherwise abused her. Another of Hammurabi's laws said that if "a woman quarrel with her husband," and she claimed he had mistreated her, "the reasons for her prejudice must be presented." If there was "no fault on her part," the statute went on, "but he leaves and neglects her, then no guilt attaches to this woman. She shall take her dowry and go back to her father's house."[21]

Other common causes for divorce were a wife's inability to have children and the unfaithfulness of either the husband or wife. If the woman was the adulterer, the penalty for her and her lover could be quite unforgiving. In Babylonia a law allowed for tying both of them hand and foot and tossing them into the river to drown. Because no records of actual divorces in the region have survived, it is uncertain how often such harsh penalties were enforced. Modern experts think that in practice many husbands and court judges likely acted more humanely and imposed lesser punishments.

Having Children

While many Mesopotamian laws dealt with marriage, dowries, and divorce, even more addressed the rights and well-being of children. This is

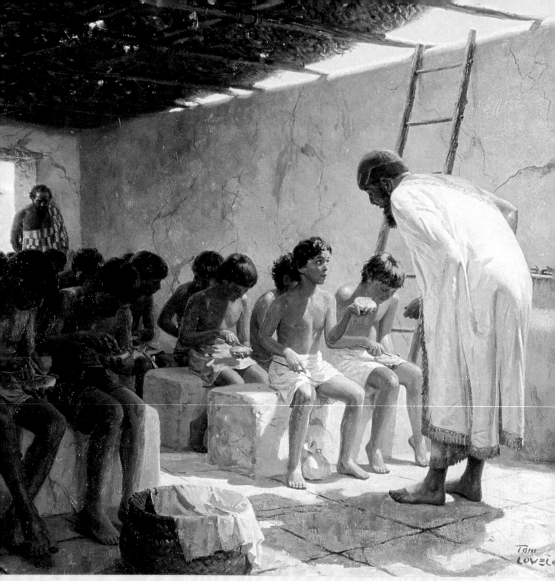

In the patriarchal societies of ancient Mesopotamia, male offspring had special importance. Where it existed, formal schooling (pictured) was open only to boys.

because children represented the community's future, and their welfare was viewed as critical. Since society was patriarchal, the security and interests of male offspring were especially important. Accordingly, when a mother gave birth to a son, the family saw reason to celebrate with extra joy.

Whether the new baby was a boy or girl, rejoicing naturally took place only when it was born alive. The sad reality was that the infant mortality rate was extremely high. Modern estimates put it at a whopping 30 percent or more, compared to less than 1 percent in modern Western countries. To blame for this were the primitive state of medical knowledge, belief in and a reliance on magic and luck, and near total ignorance about prenatal care. For instance, people thought that much of childbirth was controlled or overseen by demons, including the hideous and savage Lamashtu, who was thought to cause miscarriages and crib death. "Prenatal care," Nemet-Nejat explains,

> involved the use of amulets, herbal potions, rituals, and incantations [chants]. Amulets were objects believed to have magical and protective power, bringing luck or averting evil. In order to produce the necessary magical effect, amulets were worn by a person or placed at a special location. A woman in labor wore the image of the demon Pazuzu to counteract the evil of Lamashtu for herself, her unborn children, and her newborn child.[22]

Assuming a child was born alive and healthy, he or she eventually began playing with toys. Among the toys discovered by archaeologists in the ruins of Mesopotamian cities are dolls and miniature furniture for young girls; miniature chariots and slingshots for young boys; and jump ropes and balls for both genders. In poorer families, especially on farms, once a child was seen as old enough to work, he or she had to put aside toys and start performing daily chores.

WORDS IN CONTEXT
amulet
An object thought to have magical powers that can protect a person against evil.

Couples who were unable to have children of their own frequently adopted at least one child, most often a boy. Not only did such couples see it as their societal duty to contribute to raising the city's next generation, they also wanted to make sure someone would be there to take care of them when they were old and infirm. Life expectancy was about forty years, and only a small minority of people lived into their fifties and beyond. The reality that people needed help in their old age is reflected in a popular proverb dating from Babylon circa 1600 BC. "The strong live by their own wages," it goes. "The weak [live] by the wages of their children."[23]

One way to adopt a child was to rescue an abandoned infant. Another way was to sign a contract with parents who were too poor to raise all their children and had decided to give one of them up. The several Mesopotamian laws pertaining to adoption always looked out for the child's interests. One of Hammurabi's statutes, for instance, provides the adopted boy an out if his new father does not properly provide for him: "If a man does not maintain a child that he has adopted as a son and reared with his other children, then his adopted son may return to his [biological] father's house."[24]

It is unlikely, however, that this law had to be applied very often. Most people who went through the trouble of adopting a son were of modest means and felt strongly that they needed him. They realized his enormous value and so were careful to nurture him. Once again, a common proverb captures one of the truths of life recognized by the residents of that singular time and place. Appearing initially in Sumerian times, it states: "A poor man does not strike his son a single blow; he treasures him forever."[25]

Chapter Three

Writing, Literature, and the Arts

Large-scale agriculture, cities, empires, and law codes were not the only innovations that the early peoples of Mesopotamia gave the world. Another was the art of writing, which first arose among the Sumerians in the late fourth millennium BC. The Sumerians, Babylonians, and Assyrians also produced the first formal literary forms, including epic poems, hymns to the gods, and diplomatic letters. The first scribes, literate individuals who made their living by writing, also appeared in ancient Mesopotamia, as did the first libraries. In addition, the early inhabitants of the Tigris-Euphrates valley were among the pioneers of what today are viewed as the fine arts of sculpture, mural painting, and mosaics.

The Beauties of Cuneiform

Of all these artistic advances, the earliest and perhaps most influential was writing. By roughly 3100 BC the first examples of writing had appeared in Ur, Uruk, and other Sumerian cities. Not long after that a sophisticated writing system, today known as cuneiform, emerged. Early modern scholars took that term from the Latin word *cuneus*, meaning "wedge-shaped," because the characters making up cuneiform look like little wedges. A person created them by pressing the triangular tip of a stiff river reed into the surface of a moist clay tablet. When the tablet dried, it hardened, rendering a permanent record of the words and ideas the person wished to convey.

One of the beauties of cuneiform was that it could be adapted to almost any language. Today the alphabet employed for the English language is also used for French, German, and several other languages. Similarly, the cuneiform characters the Sumerians invented to express their language was later adopted by the Babylonians and Assyrians to communicate their own tongue—Akkadian. After Sumerian ceased to be spoken widely in the early second millennium BC, Akkadian became the main language of correspondence and diplomacy in Mesopotamia.

No matter which language one desired to convey, the art of writing revolutionized human life. First, it was now possible to keep detailed, permanent financial records and inventories of goods. Second, people could write down long, detailed messages and send them via couriers to individuals situated many miles away. That eliminated the need for messengers to try to memorize and recite such communications. Moreover, all sorts of information, from lists of former kings and existing laws to food recipes and data about the movements of the planets, could be recorded in writing.

The High-Status Scribes

The only major drawback of the cuneiform writing system was that it was very complex and therefore difficult and time-consuming to learn and use.

For that reason, few people in Mesopotamian society became literate. Rather, writing became a specialized skill practiced only by members of an elite group of men (and on occasion a few women) called scribes. Anyone who needed to write a letter, make a list, or keep track of inventory hired a scribe to do the job. Not surprisingly, the scribes also came to dominate the area of advanced education, which relied heavily on literacy.

> **WORDS IN CONTEXT**
> *dubsar*
> The Sumerian word for a scribe.

The Sumerian word for a scribe was *dubsar*, while Akkadian speakers called a scribe a *tupsharru*. No matter what they were called, scribes held key positions in society. They committed to writing official decrees, diplomatic letters, and old and new laws for the government; created precious written versions of traditional hymns and prayers for the temple

The wedge-shaped characters of cuneiform writing create a permanent record of some aspect of life in Sumeria thousands of years ago. Although developed by the Sumerians, cuneiform was adopted by other cultures.

priests; and kept financial accounts for the palace, temple estates, and well-to-do merchants. "There was also a demand," Gwendolyn Leick writes, "for specially commissioned literary works to commemorate the dedication of statues or the restoration of buildings."[26] All these services required the skills of scribes.

Because they had such special abilities, scribes were widely respected. So government officials, priests, and other high-placed individuals sometimes gave them various supervisory duties. A short passage has survived in which an actual scribe describes some of these duties:

> Let me explain to you carefully the art of being a scribe, since you have mentioned it. You have put me in charge over your house and never have I let you find me idling about. I held the slaves, slave girls, and the rest of [the workers in] your household to their tasks, saw to it that they enjoyed their bread, clothing, [and] that they work properly. . . . [I] made the men work [in the fields], a challenging task which permits me no sleep either by night or in the heat of the day.[27]

A few unusually ambitious scribes took advantage of their literacy and high social status to gain political influence and even considerable power. The most successful known example was Assyria's King Ashurbanipal, who reigned from about 668 to about 627 BC. He began as a scribe and worked his way up through the complex of palace officials to the very top. One of the inscriptions he composed with his own hands has survived. "I studied the secret lore of the entire scribal craft," he boasts.

> I know the celestial and terrestrial portents. I discussed with confidence in the circle of the master [scribes]. . . . I can solve the most complicated divisions and multiplications which do not have a solution. I have read intricate tablets inscribed with obscure Sumerian and Akkadian [texts, which are] difficult to unravel, and examined sealed, obscure, and confused inscriptions on stone from before the flood.[28]

Scribal skills were so highly respected that whoever managed to master them, regardless of gender, could gain increased social status. This is proved by the existence of a handful of female scribes in the region. Among them were the nun-like followers of the sun god Utu, women who kept extensive written records in their temples. The name of one

In Their Own Words

The Queen of Earth and Heaven

Among the more important and popular ancient Mesopotamian hymns was the one excerpted here, dedicated to Inanna, goddess of love and war.

I am Inanna! Which god compares with me? [The chief god] Enlil gave me the heavens and he gave me the Earth. I am Inanna! He gave me lordship, and he gave me queenship. He gave me battles and he gave me fighting. He gave me the storm-wind and he gave me the dust cloud. He placed the heavens on my head as a crown. He put the Earth at my feet as sandals. He wrapped [a] holy [robe] around my body. He put the holy scepter in my hand. The [other] gods are [like] small birds, but I am the falcon. . . . When I enter the Ekur, the house of Enlil, the gate-keeper does not lift his hand against my breast. The minister does not tell me, "Rise!" The heavens are mine and the Earth is mine. I am heroic! Which god compares with me?

Quoted in University of Oxford (UK) Faculty of Oriental Studies, *Electronic Text Corpus of Sumerian Literature*. http://etcsl.orinst.ox.ac.uk.

female scribe has survived the ravages of time—Enheduanna, daughter of the renowned Akkadian monarch Sargon the Great. She became better educated than most men in his empire. He made her high priestess of the temple of Nanna, the moon god, at Ur, where she composed many poems, some of which have survived.

Lofty but Entertaining Epics

Poetry was only one of many literary fields that evolved in early Mesopotamia following the emergence of writing. Over time a wide array of poetic genres developed, of which the longest, most complex, and most popular was epic poetry. The Sumerians and Babylonians turned out dozens of epics, all of which exploited serious, universal themes such as the creation of the universe, death, loyalty, divine intervention in human affairs, and love. In summary, Stephen Bertman says, these themes "are the great deeds of human beings and the gods, and the intertwined existence of their worlds."[29]

Those lofty tales were more than well written and entertaining in their own day. Several of them also strongly influenced the mythology and literature of later peoples, including the Hebrews, Greeks, and other precursors of Western civilization. Probably the most familiar example is the story of the great flood, which appears in more than one Sumerian epic. A Babylonian version of it made its way into the Hebrew scriptures, which became the Old Testament, which in turn became part of the Christian Bible.

The most famous of the Mesopotamian epics, a story widely beloved by everyone in the region—young and old, rich and poor, and of all ethnic backgrounds—was the tale of the great hero Gilgamesh. He experienced a series of exciting adventures while searching for the secret of immortality. He finally found it, but soon afterward made a mistake that allowed it to slip through his fingers.

A close second in importance to Gilgamesh's tale among the epics was the mighty *Epic of Creation*. Known to the Babylonians as the *Enuma Elish* (meaning "when on high"), it was seen as a sort of historical document as well as a sacred story to be revered and repeated. In other words, people believed that the god Marduk actually created the existing world in the manner told in the epic. The work was so admired and honored that special performers recited it aloud in public each year during Babylonia's New Year's festival.

Sacred Texts and the First Libraries

In addition to epic poems, the people of Mesopotamia enjoyed numerous other literary works. Especially important to the average person were sacred texts, including hymns to the gods. Most hymns were probably initially composed and memorized by priests to be used in public religious festivals. Once these pieces were written down, they were copied, and after that anyone who knew how to read could recite them to people who lacked that skill.

Modern experts view such hymns of praise to the gods as particularly valuable because they provide basic facts about the attributes, powers, and accomplishments of those divinities. A clear example is one of the most beautiful of all the surviving Mesopotamian hymns, dedicated to Shamash, the Babylonian sun god (Utu to the Sumerians). Dating from the early second millennium BC, it reads in part,

> You climb to the mountains surveying the earth, you suspend from the heavens the circle of the lands. You care for all the peoples of the lands, and everything that Ea, king of the counselors, had created is entrusted to you. Whatever has breath you shepherd without exception. You are their keeper in upper and lower regions. Regularly and without cease you traverse the heavens. Every day you pass over the broad earth. . . . Shepherd of that beneath, keeper of that above, you, Shamash, are the light of everything.[30]

Archaeologists have unearthed random examples of these types of works in ruined houses, temples, palaces, and other ancient buildings. A majority of surviving examples, however, were found in the region's ancient archives, often called libraries. (In such cases the word *library* can be misleading. Average Mesopotamians were not allowed to borrow books and other documents from the archives, as people do from modern libraries.) One of the larger archives, containing several thousand texts on clay tablets, was found at Mari, an important city in western Mesopotamia.

A good deal larger was the archive of King Ashurbanipal, the former scribe, in his magnificent capital of Nineveh. With more than twenty thousand tablets (of which about five thousand have been translated), "it has every right to be called the first systematically collected library in the ancient Middle East,"[31] states scholar A. Leo Oppenheim. Ashurbanipal wrote the dedication of the collection himself, saying in part, "The wisdom of Nabu, the signs of writing, as many as have been devised, I wrote on tablets, I arranged in series, I collated, and for my royal inspection and recital, I placed them in my palace."[32]

Proverbs, Fables, and Lamentations

Of the many kinds of literature contained in Mesopotamia's archives, the broadest category was secular, or nonreligious, texts. Included were proverbs and other wise sayings, erotic poems, royal inscriptions, lamentations (sad comments or songs), personal letters, educational texts, medical and astrological texts, and historical accounts.

Proverbs (brief, wise sayings) were generally passed along from one generation to another. At first this happened orally. Sometime in the second millennium BC, however, scribes began creating written collections of proverbs. People in those days felt that these examples of so-called "wisdom literature" tended to capture basic truths of the human condition. That they were right is confirmed by the fact that numerous Mesopotamian proverbs are no less meaningful today. A good example is the Sumerian saying, "Wealth is hard to come by, but poverty is always at hand." Another Sumerian proverb, "He who eats too much will not be able to sleep,"[33] also still rings true, as does the later Babylonian saying, "If you go and take the field of an enemy, the enemy will come and take your field."[34]

> **WORDS IN CONTEXT**
> **lamentation**
> A sad commentary or song, most often about the death of a king or fall of a city.

Proverbs were often lighthearted and sometimes humorous. So were examples of another popular kind of wisdom literature—fables, short tales that satirized, or poked fun at, common social situations. More serious and somber were lamentations (or laments), poems that observed a person's death or the fall of a city or nation. Several of the surviving Mesopotamian lamentations incorporate real details about a king's death or a city's demise and therefore have value to modern historians. An outstanding example is the *Lamentation Over the Destruction of Ur*.

Composed not long after 2000 BC, it marks the fall of the last of the Sumerian empire, dubbed the Third Dynasty of Ur, or Ur-III, by modern scholars. The part of the lament that follows sounds like an actual eyewitness account of the dreadful aftermath of wartime slaughter:

> On that day did the storm [of war] leave the country. The people mourn. Its people's corpses, not potsherds, littered the approaches. The walls were gaping. The high gates, the roads, were piled with dead. In the wide streets, where feasting crowds once gathered, jumbled they lay. In all the streets and roadways bodies lay. In open fields that used to fill with dancers, the people lay in heaps.[35]

Letters

The ancient Mesopotamian libraries also contained many personal letters, including ones written by one ruler to another. When an ordinary, illiterate person wanted to send someone a letter, he hired a scribe and dictated the message to him. In addition to those letters carved onto clay

Within the magnificent capital of Nineveh (pictured) existed a huge library of twenty thousand cuneiform tablets. This archive represented the works collected by Assyria's King Ashurbanipal, a former scribe.

Looking Back

Gilgamesh's Lost Lines Unearthed

British researcher George Smith made the first English translation of the *Epic of Gilgamesh* in 1872. At the time, fifteen of the poem's thirty-five hundred lines were still missing. Hoping to find them, Smith oversaw a major expedition to Iraq. Incredibly, by sheer unexpected luck he found the lost lines after only a few weeks of searching. He later recounted how one evening he "sat down to examine" some cuneiform writings unearthed in "the day's digging." After "brushing off the earth from the fragments to read their contents," he was surprised and overjoyed to find that they

> contained the greater portion of seventeen lines of inscription belonging to the first column of the [Babylonian] account of the Deluge [great flood], and fitting into the only place where there was a serious blank in the [Gilgamesh] story. When I had first published the account of this tablet I had conjectured that there were about fifteen lines wanting [lacking] in this part of the story, and now with this portion I was enabled to make it nearly complete.

Quoted in C.W. Ceram, ed., *Hands on the Past: Pioneer Archaeologists Tell Their Own Story*. New York: Knopf, 1966, p. 250.

tablets, over time some came to be written on animal hide, papyrus (paper made from a river plant), or other perishable materials.

Such letters followed a standard form, just as modern ones do. But instead of the familiar salutations "Dear X" or "Dear Mr. X," the most common Mesopotamian version was "X says the following: Tell Y that. . . ." Next, the letter writer stated that he hoped the recipient was in good health. If the letter writer was a member of a lower social class than the recipient, he used subservient phrases such as "I grovel at your feet." In contrast, if the two were social equals, the letter writer addressed the recipient as "brother." Finally, if the writer had a higher social status than the recipient, it was common for the text to have a curt, unfriendly sounding tone, as if taking time to address the recipient was beneath the writer's dignity.

Extraordinarily Gifted Individuals

While scribes and other literate people were admired and respected in ancient Mesopotamia, those with what today are seen as artistic talents were not. Society viewed someone who sculpted statues, painted murals, or created mosaics as just another craftsman, akin to a potter or metalsmith. As such, they labored under a lowly social status and for very little pay.

Although it is many centuries too late to benefit those artists of the distant past, the modern world has come to see them for what they were—extraordinarily gifted individuals. This can be seen by the surviving remnants of the handiwork of Sumerian and Babylonian sculptors and especially that of their Assyrian counterparts, who were among the greatest sculptors of the ancient world.

Assyrian sculptors worked in two main disciplines, or categories. One was freestanding, three-dimensional statues, and the other was reliefs (or bas-reliefs), carved scenes raised somewhat from flat surfaces. Of the freestanding statues, the biggest and most visually stunning are the giant human-headed bulls that guarded the entrances to the Assyrian palaces. People called them *lamassi* (or *lamassu*), meaning "bull-men," as well as *aladlammu*, or "protective spirits." Each, exhibiting a long beard and eye-catching wings, weighs close to 20 tons (18 metric tons).

> **WORDS IN CONTEXT**
> *lamassi*
> "Bull-men"; the huge carved stone bulls that guarded the entrances of ancient Assyrian palaces.

The finest of the Assyrian relief sculptures are the long panels originally mounted on the walls of the royal palaces. Carved from gypsum and occasionally other kinds of stone, they display military battles, hunting expeditions, large-scale building projects, and other proud accomplishments of the Assyrian rulers. "In the scenes of hunting," historian Chester G. Starr states, "animals were shown with more realism than had ever before been achieved. Here the artists gave a vivid sense of motion, even at times of pity for the dying lions or wild asses."[36] These sculpted panels are not just decorative art of very high quality. They are also a type of propaganda intended to impress both Assyrian subjects and foreign visitors.

No less impressive are some of the murals that Mesopotamian artisans painted on the walls of palaces, temples, and the houses of the rich and famous. A number of these works have survived in varying states of preservation. Some of the finest were found in Mari in the ruins of the palace of King Zimri-Lim, who ruled from about 1775 to about 1761 BC. One of the murals shows the king pronouncing an oath beside Ishtar, goddess of love and protector of royal monarchs. Around the two main figures, the artist or artists painted striking images of other gods, along with griffins, mythical creatures that signified both kingly and divine authority.

As he began work on such a mural, the painter first coated the wall with plaster consisting of a mix of mud and powdered lime or gypsum. After the plaster dried, the artist used a pointed tool to sketch the outlines of the scene. Then he applied the paint. This "dry-surface" method was used throughout the third millennium BC and most of the following one. In the late second millennium BC, painters began employing the fresco method, in which they applied their paint to wet plaster. A significant advantage of this approach is that the paint and plaster dry together, thereby merging and making the colors last longer.

WORDS IN CONTEXT

fresco

A painting method in which the paint is applied to a surface coated in wet plaster.

Mosaics and Cylinder Seals

Mosaic artists were also in demand in ancient Mesopotamia. A mosaic is a picture created by gluing numerous small colored tiles, pieces of glass, stones, shells, or other objects to a surface. The classic, and today most often photographed early example of Mesopotamian mosaic, is the renowned Royal Standard of Ur (or simply the Standard of Ur). It appears to have been made in the mid–third millennium BC. Now on display in London's British Museum, this splendid work is essentially a wooden box about 19.5 inches (50 cm) long, 8.5 inches (21 cm) wide, and overlaid with thousands of small bits of shell, red limestone, and blue lapis lazuli. The scenes on the box's surfaces portray a Sumerian military victory and the festivities following it. Importantly, the costumes, weapons, tools, and other artifacts depicted are all rendered with the utmost accuracy, a boon to modern scholars. The late, renowned English archaeologist Seton Lloyd aptly said of the Standard of Ur, "As an introduction to the dress, appearance, and behavior of the Sumerians, this is a remarkably revealing document."[37]

The Royal Standard of Ur, a famous early example of Mesopotamian mosaic, depicts a Sumerian military victory and the celebration that followed. The artwork presents a remarkably realistic view of the clothing, tools, and weapons of the period.

Still another important art form in the region was the cylinder seal, a decorative object that Mesopotamian artisans turned out possibly by the millions. Each was a small piece of stone—or bronze, copper, gold, ivory, shell, or bone—on which individuals called seal-cutters carved pictures, patterns, or words. Cylinder seals were used to create small raised images, or stamps, that were equivalent to personal signatures on modern documents. One made such a stamp by pressing and rolling a seal into moist clay.

To manufacture the miniature scenes and/or messages on cylinder seals, the seal-cutters used chisels, knife blades, hand-turned metal drills, and other small tools. Those scenes often illustrated episodes from well-known myths or events from everyday life, such as people worshipping the gods, dancing, feasting, riding in boats, or planting crops. The most universal theme, Lloyd explains, "is conflict—usually between lions and the mythical protectors of flocks and herds, which they have attacked. Two figures—a 'naked hero' and a 'bull-man'—appear with great frequency as protectors and have often been identified with the characters of Gilgamesh and his companion Enkidu of the famous epic." Eventually, Lloyd goes on, Sumerian seal-carving "attained an unprecedented degree of artistic accomplishment. It reached a yet higher standard of perfection in Akkadian times, when the scope of the subject was dramatically widened, the seal-cutter appearing undaunted by the complexity of the religious scenes he was expected to compress into so small a space."[38]

Cylinder seals were common, inexpensive objects on the one hand and artistic masterpieces on the other. This reality was among many dual or opposing aspects of life in Mesopotamia. Another was the fact that artistic geniuses earned little money, respect, and recognition for their talents. Still another was that most people in society were either very poor or very rich. Such disparities and imperfections were bound to exist in a place where peoples and societies constantly experimented with and struggled to perfect a relatively new concept called civilization.

Chapter Four

Gods and
Religious Beliefs

The vast majority of ancient Mesopotamians were polytheistic, meaning they believed in and worshipped a wide array of gods. Religious concepts and rituals pervaded the lives of Sumerians, Babylonians, and Assyrians alike, from the poorest peasants to the wealthiest, most exalted monarchs. People both prayed at home and took part in religious observances in the streets during sacred holidays, of which there were many. Also, every town, without exception, had one or more temples, which were large-scale institutions. Local priests and their temple compounds and farming estates wielded enormous social and economic influence as well as spiritual authority.

Moreover, many of the religious ideas accepted by the average Mesopotamian went on to profoundly influence the lore and beliefs of later ancient faiths, among them Judaism and Christianity. As Samuel N. Kramer tells it, "Mesopotamia's rich complex of ritual and myth" in many ways helped to shape early Western religion:

The Mesopotamian notion that water was the source of all creation found its way, for instance, into the Genesis account of the creation of the world, and the Biblical view that man was fashioned of clay and imbued with the "breath of life" goes back to Mesopotamian roots. So, too, does the Biblical concept that man was created primarily to serve God and that God's creative power is in His Word. The idea that catastrophes are divine punishment for wrongdoing and that pain and suffering must be submitted to patiently, also have striking Mesopotamian parallels.[39]

Inventing the Gods

These complex and appealing religious concepts that so heavily influenced later faiths did not appear suddenly and fully formed in Mesopotamia. Rather, views of the nature of the divine changed considerably over time in the region. Furthermore, it took centuries for the Sumerian religious faith to evolve into its mature form.

Before and throughout most of the Ubaidian period (circa 5000–3500 BC), it appears that the prevailing beliefs in the area were animistic. Animism is a religious system that holds that large numbers of invisible spirits, some of them good, others evil, exist everywhere in nature. An animist thinks that these spirits, which tend to be more like forces than beings with concrete personalities, inhabit mountains, rocks, trees, rivers, and even the sky.

Sumerians bring a gilded statue to their temple. Temples had a prominent place in the cities of ancient Mesopotamia, and religious observances grew out of a rich mix of myth and ritual.

Evidence indicates that as the centuries wore on, these nature spirits increasingly acquired human-like intelligence, emotions, and behaviors. As this happened, worshippers also steadily endowed those natural forces with human form. The reasons for these developments remain a bit unclear. But most modern experts believe it was because people pictured the divine entities as having the ability to think and to act based on that thinking. Humans appeared to be the only living things in the world who could think. Thus, it seemed only logical that any divine forces that could think must also display human shape and emotions.

Still, worshippers recognized that these forces went beyond average human-like attributes. In order to control all of nature, the world, and the human race, the gods must be somehow *super*human. "The mighty beings in charge of the universe," in Kramer's words, "must be more powerful and effective than their human counterparts on Earth. And these beings must live forever, for the unthinkable alternative was utter confusion at their death." Moreover, Kramer notes, logic also dictated that

> **WORDS IN CONTEXT**
> **pantheon**
> A group of gods worshipped by a people, nation, or religious faith.

there had to be many such gods to guide the innumerable physical and spiritual components of the world, and the Mesopotamians had no difficulty in supplying this need by inventing new gods when the occasion arose. The surviving documents show that, even by 2500 BC, the role call of Sumerian gods, the pantheon, consisted of thousands of deities, each with its own name and sphere of activity.[40]

Major and Minor Gods

Also by the mid-2000s BC, Sumerian society had amassed a large number of myths associated with the members of the divine pantheon. The leader of the gods, Enlil, for instance, appeared in several mythical tales with plots and themes that illustrated his divine roles and deeds. The most crucial of these were the colorful stories telling how he organized the universe and natural elements and eventually fashioned humans.

In a very real sense, Enlil and his fellow Sumerian gods went on to outlive the Sumerians themselves. This was because the Babylonians and Assyrians, who in the second millennium BC inherited Sumerian culture, absorbed the Sumerian gods and their roles and myths. Only superficial changes, such as names and a few minor personal attributes, were made in the older divine roster. The result was that when Babylonian culture flourished in the second and first millennia BC, the chief Babylonian god—Marduk—was equivalent in many ways to the Sumerian deity Enlil. (Enlil also passed into Babylonian times as Ellil, a lesser weather god.)

Besides the chief deity, Enlil/Marduk, the Mesopotamian pantheon featured several others that were widely respected and worshipped. Particularly prominent was the Sumerian Utu, god of the sun, whom the Babylonians called Shamash. "In their reverence," a Babylonian hymn to that god proclaims, people and nations praise "the mention of you, and worship your majesty forever." The hymn goes on to call Shamash "brightener of gloom, illuminator of darkness, dispeller of darkness," and "illuminator of the broad earth."[41] Clearly, all Mesopotamians recognized how important the sun and its light and warmth were to the world and living things. So a significant portion of the region's rituals, hymns, and myths were directed at the heavenly being thought to embody that blindingly bright disk.

Other major Mesopotamian deities included the Sumerian moon god Nanna (Sin to the Babylonians) and Inanna (the Babylonian Ishtar), goddess of love and sexual passion. Ishtar had other important attributes and associations. On the one hand, she was a warrior goddess, and on the other, people identified her with the "evening star," the planet Venus. Meanwhile, the Sumerian Enki (Babylonian Ea) oversaw all waters that flowed above and below the ground. Accordingly, artists often showed streams of water spraying out of his shoulders or from a pottery vessel he held in his hands. People also viewed Enki/Ea as a deity who dispensed wisdom and protected craft workers.

In addition to these and about a dozen other major gods, the residents of Mesopotamia recognized numerous minor deities and supernatural

In Their Own Words

Balasi's Report to the King

One of the many religious rituals practiced by ancient Mesopotamian priests was divination, predicting future events by studying natural phenomena such as the organs and behavior of animals. A surviving Assyrian text contains a description of a real example of divination in the palace of King Esarhaddon, who ruled between 680 and 669 BC. The king had witnessed some ravens acting strangely and requested that his leading diviner, named Balasi, study and interpret the behavior. The priest soon reported to Esarhaddon and said,

> To the king, my lord Esarhaddon, from your servant Balasi: Good health to your majesty! May the gods Nabu and Marduk bless your Majesty. As to Your Majesty's request addressed to me concerning the incident with the ravens, here are the relevant omens: "If a raven brings something into a person's house, this man will obtain something that does not belong to him. If a falcon or a raven drops something he is carrying upon a person's house or in front of a man, this house will have much traffic, [and] traffic means profit. If a bird carries meat, another bird, or anything else, and drops it upon a person's house, this man will obtain a large inheritance.

Quoted in A. Leo Oppenheim, ed., *Letters from Mesopotamia: Official, Business, and Private Letters on Clay Tablets from Two Millennia.* Chicago: University of Chicago Press, 1967, pp. 166–67.

beings. Some of them congregated in and were worshipped in groups. One such group—the Igigi—numbering perhaps three hundred or more, were what might be called heavenly helpers because they carried out menial, or unskilled and tedious, work for the more important members of the pantheon.

Another group of secondary divinities, the Anunnaki (or Annunaki), also did various jobs, including military missions, for the major gods. It is not mere chance that the Anunnaki were very similar to the angels that populate the Hebrew/Christian Old Testament. During the mid–first millennium BC, a large group of Hebrews were captured by a Babylonian army and resettled in the heart of Mesopotamia. Modern historians believe that among the ranks of these transplants were the authors of some written narratives that later became books of the Bible. While in the Tigris-Euphrates valley, those Hebrews were exposed to local religious concepts and seem to have adopted some of them, including the Anunnaki. In the Old Testament the angels that so strongly resemble them are called the Jedi, or Nephilim. (In turn, filmmaker George Lucas adapted the Jedi for his *Star Wars* movies, making them a band of stalwart knights who fight against evil. This is only one of many ways that various aspects of ancient Mesopotamian culture have quietly followed a twisting path into modern culture.)

Bringing Order to Human Life

In Mesopotamian religious lore, the Igigi, Anunnaki, and other minor deities were earlier created by Enlil/Marduk and a handful of major gods. The latter also created the human race, and nearly all the gods had an intense interest in human affairs. So concerned were the heavenly beings with life in the Mesopotamian cities that they made a set of regulations to bring divinely inspired order to human life. The Sumerians called these rules *me*, while the Babylonians and Assyrians referred to them as *parsu*. The *me* guided numerous aspects of civilization. According to Stephen Bertman, they included "government

> **WORDS IN CONTEXT**
> *me*
> A series of divinely inspired rules designed to bring order to society.

The Babylonian goddess Ishtar (or Inanna to the Sumerians) guided love and sexual passion. She was also viewed as a warrior goddess.

and religion, war and peace, sexual intercourse (including prostitution), art and music, and crafts and professions, as well as such abstractions as truth and falsehood, and sadness and joy."[42]

One way that average people learned about the *me* and the importance of following them was through telling and retelling popular myths. Especially instructive was the tale in which the lofty Enlil himself broke one of the sacred rules. In the story, he was walking in the woods one day and came upon the lovely young goddess Ninlil, who was swimming naked in a pond. Enlil proceeded to rape her, thereby going against the civilized societal order personified by the *me*.

When the other gods heard what had occurred, they were horribly disappointed with Enlil. Not only had he sinned, they said, he had also betrayed the very rules he had created to make life better and more secure. One of the surviving written versions of the myth says, "The fifty great gods and the seven gods who decide destinies had Enlil arrested [and] Enlil, the ritually impure, left the city."[43] To ensure that the *me* did not thereafter become meaningless, those divine judges told Enlil that he had to accept a stiff penalty. Now thinking more clearly, he fully agreed, apologized, and allowed them to banish him to the underworld. (Ninlil became pregnant from the rape and soon afterward gave birth to the moon god Nanna. In order that the latter deity would be raised by both his parents, the mother and child followed Enlil into the underworld.)

From this solemn but vivid myth, the average Mesopotamian learned the importance of making sure people followed the *me*. The story showed that even the god who had helped to create the rules of right and wrong had been punished for breaking one of them. That implied that any mere mortal who sinned would surely seriously suffer for it.

The rules of order inspired by the gods and gratefully followed by the Sumerians and many later Mesopotamians were also affected by a special, magical (though in reality quite imaginary) object. People came to call it the Tablet of Destiny. Fashioned by divine hands, it was thought to contain written accounts of the future deeds and fates of both the gods and humans. Moreover, any person who managed to acquire the tablet would suddenly possess superhuman powers. This explains why a number of Mesopotamian myths featured people trying to steal the tablet.

Looking Back

Taking Comfort in a Troubled World

The *me* (*parsu* to the Babylonians and Assyrians) defined how devout individuals should properly conduct themselves during religious rituals as well as in everyday life. The late, noted scholar of ancient Mesopotamia Samuel N. Kramer adds that the *me* were

a response to their yearning for reassurance in a troubling world. They needed to believe that the universe and all its parts, once created, would continue to operate in an orderly and effective manner, not subject to disintegration and deterioration. The *me*, devised by Enlil, governed everyone and everything in the universe. And mortal men could take comfort in the knowledge that the blue sky, the teeming earth, the dark Underworld, the wild sea, were all acting in accordance with the rules of the gods. There were more than a hundred *me*, one for each of the aspects of the world and its civilization. There were special *me* for deities and men, lands and cities, palaces and temples, love and law, truth and falsehood, war and peace, music and art, cult and ritual, as well as for all crafts and professions. Enlil granted these *me* to guide the gods, spelling out their rights, duties, and privileges, bounds and controls, authority and restraint.

Samuel N. Kramer, *Cradle of Civilization*. New York: Time-Life, 1978, p. 102.

A third facet of divinely inspired order in Mesopotamian life, one that everyone, whether rich or poor, could easily relate to, was the idea of the personal god. People believed that each person had a deity that watched over him or her. That individual was allowed, and even encouraged, to pray to this divine mentor anytime and anywhere.

The way that someone selected his or her personal god is no longer clear. However, evidence has been found that shows that certain deities were patrons, or protectors, of various social and occupational groups, including soldiers, farmers, craft workers, and children. There were also personal gods of entire towns and cities. The belief was that a city's divine patron took a keen interest in that community and its inhabitants and watched over them.

After-Death Dealings

The place where Enlil went as a penalty for raping Ninlil, identified as the underworld in most surviving versions of the myth, was not the equivalent of the hell envisioned by modern Christians. In fact, a majority of ancient Mesopotamians did not accept the notion that people received punishments or rewards after death based on their earthly behavior. Instead, says Gwendolyn Leick,

> they were more inclined to interpret misfortune, illness, and of course death itself as a form of punishment for "sin." They grieved for the dead, lamenting their passing as Gilgamesh does in the epic when [his friend] Enkidu dies. But they accepted death as the "fate of mankind." They preferred to bury the deceased within the family compound, below the thick mud-brick walls, or beneath the floor of a little-used room. Sometimes [they placed the bodies] in clay coffins, with few if any grave-goods. Thus, the ancestors remained part of the house and it was convenient to offer them their daily libations [liquid sacrifices] of water, a duty that the male heirs performed.[44]

That does not mean that the Sumerians and other peoples of the region rejected the concepts of the afterlife and underworld. Some of their writings reveal that they did accept that a person's soul might go somewhere after that individual died. They called it by different names, among them the Land of No Return, the Great Earth, and the Land of the Dead. This place had divine rulers, the grim-faced goddess Ereshkigal and her consort (companion), the god Nergal. Myths claim that they dwelled in a palace made of lapis lazuli and other precious stones.

Unlike the Christian hell or heaven, however, the Mesopotamian Land of No Return was not a place where people either suffered eternal punishments or enjoyed paradise with the divine. Instead, a deceased person's soul found itself on the mostly featureless plains surrounding Ereshkigal and Nergal's palace. There the soul simply existed forever and ever, feeling neither joy nor sorrow, pleasure nor pain.

Another uninviting aspect of Mesopotamian after-death dealings was the widespread belief that ghosts sometimes rose from the dead and intimidated the living. People thought that these spirits returned to the earth's surface at certain special times of the year, and especially during the annual celebration called the "return of the dead." It took place in the month the Babylonians called Abu (July/August).

The belief was that the ghosts desired to haunt and terrorize the living. But if they did so, the great god Shamash penalized them somehow. So apparently, during the holiday many of these phantoms just floated around harmlessly, and when the festival ended they flew back down to the Land of No Return. Still, the threat that an irate god might allow ghosts and zombies to run amok among the living was ever present in people's minds. Many recalled Ereshkigal's angry words of warning in a popular epic: "I shall raise up the dead, and they will eat the living. I shall make the dead outnumber the living!"[45]

The Rituals of Worship

Based largely on their rather dreary view of life after death, most ancient Mesopotamians taught their children that they should make the best they could of their earthly lives. They should make earnest efforts to be upright, honest, constructive citizens and treat their neighbors with respect and decency. That way, the brief span of time they existed on the earth would not be wasted.

Yet the belief that no significant punishments for wrongdoing occurred after death did not mean that the gods turned a blind eye to human dishonesty and criminal activity. It has been established that the common belief was that the gods could and did mete out punishments to people *during* their lifetimes. Disease, painful deformities, blindness, and consistent bad luck were only some of these forms of divine retribution for sin.

The best way to avoid such afflictions and remain on the gods' good side was to stay out of trouble and offer the heavenly beings regular worship. The latter included the ritual of prayer. Worship also featured sacrifice, consisting of various material offerings to the gods. The most common ones were forms of nourishment such as animal flesh, fruits and other plant products, and liquids such as milk, wine, and water. Although official priests performed many sacrifices, practically anyone could do so, and family members frequently engaged in prayer and sacrifice in their homes.

Average worshippers also showed their respect for the gods by supporting their local temples and taking part in the large-scale ceremonies the temple priests conducted during religious holidays.

> **WORDS IN CONTEXT**
> **cult image**
> The statue of a god that stood in the sacred interior of a temple.

Mesopotamian temples were unlike modern churches, synagogues, and mosques in one major way. Ordinary people were not allowed to enter a temple's interior chambers where the statues of the gods—called cult images—stood. Only priests or priestesses and the king could enter those sacred rooms. There the priests tended to the holy statues, offering them daily sacrifices; performed purification rites intended to scare away evil or impurity; and interpreted various omens, signs thought to reveal the will of or messages from the gods. The gender of the clergy who carried out these tasks depended on the gender of the deity being worshipped. With a few rare exceptions, male priests catered to male gods and female priestesses attended goddesses.

The inhabitants of Babylon celebrate New Year's Day. The celebration of the New Year in ancient Mesopotamia coincided with the harvest and included prayers, the sacrifice of animals, feasting, and parades.

The Power of Religion

During the big religious festivals, many of the priests and priestesses came out of the temples and performed special rituals before crowds of ordinary worshippers. A good example is what happened during the largest festival of all. The Sumerian word for it was *Akiti*, and the Babylonians and Assyrians called it *Akitu*. Held at harvest time in the month of Nisan (March), it was a major celebration of the fruits of agriculture, society's primary food source. Ancient Mesopotamia's New Year occurred during harvest time. So people came to celebrate it, too, as part of a dual holiday.

By the early second millennium BC, the festival lasted twelve days. Following a set series of rituals, most people prayed, sacrificed animals, and feasted during the first six days. The last six days witnessed lavish formal parades through the streets of the urban centers. Thousands of worshippers marched and sang hymns while priests carried the divine cult images on splendidly decorated wagons. At some point there was a large-scale recitation of the entire *Epic of Creation*. All during the reading, the gathered multitudes stood in utter silence in a show of respect for the gods, who, many believed, were actually present in their midst.

At another dramatic moment in the festival, the Babylonian king entered a sacred outdoor enclosure. There a priest removed the ruler's crown and royal robes and suddenly slapped him hard across the face. The humbled king then knelt down and swore that he had not abused the great authority the gods had bestowed on him. This ceremony was intended to demonstrate that even kings were subject to the will and the wrath of the gods. For that single moment, once each year, the mighty monarch whose will was law was reduced to the level of the most lowly of his subjects. Such was the power of religion in a culture in which belief that invisible superbeings were always watching was nearly universal and absolute.

Chapter Five

Science, Technology, and Travel

The ancient Mesopotamians did not understand the idea of science the way the world does today. Modern scientists employ the scientific method, which produces theories based on tangible, measurable evidence. Sumerian and Babylonian thinkers did not openly search for what makes nature work, advance theories about it, and subject those ideas to rigorous experimentation to find the truth. The first thinkers who studied science using such a modern approach were a handful of Greeks who lived in the mid–first millennium BC.

Still, those early Greek scientists frequently based their ideas on ones they borrowed from the lands lying southeast of Greece, especially Babylonia. The Babylonians of that era had long traditions of using mathematics and compiling information about the moon, planets, and other heavenly bodies. Going all the way back to the Sumerians, Mesopotamian observers and researchers saw what they felt were meaningful patterns among the stars in the night sky. The Greeks inherited the shapes and themes of these constellations, among them those making up the zodiac. This was only one of many areas in which the Greeks used data and basic concepts invented in Mesopotamia.

Also long before the Greeks, the early peoples of Mesopotamia pioneered a number of key basic technological developments. These included metal tools and weapons, the wheel, wagons, chariots, and advanced siege devices. At first, such innovations made fighting more deadly, conquest more widespread, and long-range travel more viable in Mesopotamia itself. Later, however, these and other aspects of technology filtered outward into other areas. For example, soon after the lightweight chariot was invented in the Tigris-Euphrates valley in the early second millennium BC, it made its way to Egypt and then to Greece and other sectors of southern Europe.

These early examples of technology and science were fairly simple. Yet some of these innovations—the wooden plow, for instance—completely revolutionized the Middle East and not long afterward much of the rest of the inhabited world. The plow made it possible for early farmers to grow considerably bigger amounts of food. In turn, a larger food supply encouraged population growth and led directly to the formation of the first towns and cities on the Mesopotamian plains.

Sky Gazers and Astrology

The plow emerged in the Middle East sometime during the prehistoric period—that is, before the advent of writing. During those same long centuries when civilization was first taking hold in the region, some people began making systematic, or regular and organized, observations of the night sky. At the time, no smog or other air pollution, nor light pollution from bright electric lights, interfered with sky gazing. So an average person on an average night could see thousands more stars than can be seen today.

Most of the stars imbedded in that huge, inky-black canopy never changed their positions from night to night. They always occupied the same spots in the age-old constellations. There were, however, a few—five to be exact—that were unusually bright and did move slowly across night's dark dome as the months rolled by. These were the "wanderers," the planets Mercury, Venus, Mars, Jupiter, and Saturn. (Today eight planets are recognized. But Uranus and Neptune are too dim to see without a telescope, and the ancients did not realize that Earth is a planet).

Mesopotamian sky observers were mostly priests who lived and worked in the urban temples. They were certain that all of nature was controlled by the gods, who were thought to dwell somewhere in the sky. So it is not surprising that those holy men came to identify the planets moving through that sky with specific gods. The reasoning was

In the Babylonian conception of heaven and Earth, the brown strip represents Earth and the blue represents the sky and the heavens. The gods were thought to dwell somewhere in the sky, and the heavenly bodies were seen as influencing life on Earth.

that, since the gods strongly influenced human life, the planets associated with those deities must also be able to affect people and their activities. This marked the origins of astrology. Now known to be a pseudo, or false, science, it proposes that the heavenly bodies influence life on Earth.

Throughout Sumerian and Babylonian times, Stephen Bertman writes, the concern of Mesopotamian sky observers "was not with astronomy as a science but with astrology as an art by which the future could be divined through the discovery of omens, good and bad, to inform political decision making and assure personal success."[46]

Thus, just as some people today read their horoscopes in the newspaper, either seriously or for fun, a cottage industry that produced horoscopes for people existed in ancient Mesopotamia. Following is part of a surviving one, which local priests did for a Greek named Aristocrates in the third century BC (when Greek kings ruled Mesopotamia).

> Year 77 Siman, [from] the 4th [day until] the last part of the night of the fifth [day], Aristocrates was born. That day, [the] Moon [was] in Leo. [The] Sun [was] in Gemini. The Moon set its face from the middle towards the top. . . . The place of Jupiter [at that time means his life will be] regular and well. He will become rich, he will grow old, [and his] days will be numerous. Venus [was with]in 4 degrees [of] Taurus. The place of Venus [means that] wherever he may go, it will be favorable [for him and] he will have sons and daughters.[47]

Careful, Accurate Records

In spite of such nonscientific facets of ancient Mesopotamian sky observations, over the course of numerous centuries Babylonian priests did keep careful records of planetary movements. For instance, they noted when Venus passed behind the sun and a while later reappeared from the other side of its disk. Also carefully notated in their records were examples of the periodic backward, or retrograde, movement of some planets; the dates and times of solar and lunar eclipses; the sudden appearance of comets and their paths across the sky; and unusual heavenly sights, such as halos of light around the moon or sun.

The Babylonian sky gazers recorded all these things on clay tablets that were stored in archives like that of King Ashurbanipal. The earliest surviving examples have been dated to roughly 1700 BC, shortly after the reign of the Babylonian lawgiver Hammurabi. Modern historians and other experts are especially interested in the "Venus tablets." These were compiled by priest-astronomers who worked for the Babylonian monarch Ammi-saduqa, who ruled from 1646 to 1626 BC. The celestial information on the tablets is valuable because it helps to date a number of events that occurred in Mesopotamia in that era.

Other celestial observations from Mesopotamia were used to make calendars that kept track of the ongoing months and years. A lunar calendar

In Their Own Words

The Royal Road Builder and Runner

The Sumerians built some of the first roads connecting cities, along with the first hostels and inns for the convenience of travelers on these highways. One of Sumeria's last kings, Shulgi (reigned 2094–2047 BC), built a road from Nippur to Ur, a distance of about 100 miles (161 km), and a series of elaborate hostels along its length. In a surviving document, he brags about these achievements as well as how he inaugurated the road by staging a public show in which he personally ran the road's entire distance on foot.

> Because I am a powerful man, rejoicing in his loins [muscles], I enlarged the footpaths, straightened the highways of the land, I made secure travel, built there "big houses" [the hostels], planted gardens alongside of them, established resting places, settled there friendly folk, so that who[ever] comes from below [the south], [or] who[ever] comes from above [the north], might refresh themselves in its cool shade. The wayfarer who travels the highway at night might find refuge there like in a well-built city. That my name be established unto distant days, that it not leave the mouths of men, that my praise be spread wide in the land, that I be eulogized [praised] in all the lands, I, the runner, rose in my strength, all set for the course. And from Nippur to Ur, I resolved to travel as if it were but a distance of one mile.

Quoted in J.B. Pritchard, *The Ancient Near East: An Anthology of Texts and Pictures*. Princeton, NJ: Princeton University Press, 2011, pp. 338–39.

that appeared in the seventh century BC divided the year into twelve lunar months. Each of them came to be associated with one of the twelve star groups, or constellations, that are together called the zodiac.

The same observations of the night sky allowed Babylonian sky-gazing priests to develop practical units for reckoning time, including hours and minutes. They divided each hour into sixty minutes and calculated that there were twelve "double hours" in each day. (Later, Greek researchers broke these down into twenty-four single hours, rendering the system employed today.) So careful and accurate were the celestial observations of Babylonian researchers that one of them, Kidinnu (or Kidenas) measured the day's length with an error of a mere four minutes.

A solar eclipse creates a spectacular show for sky watchers. The sky watchers of ancient Babylon kept careful records of planetary movements, the passage of comets, and the dates and times of solar and lunar eclipses.

Simple and Complex Counting Systems

According to ancient documents, Kidinnu excelled in math as well as observing the heavens. This is not surprising, as math and astronomy are closely linked today as well. Indeed, both Sumerian and Babylonian mathematicians made important contributions to the practical use of complex numbers. Moreover some of their math figures and relationships are still widely used today.

One major example is the decimal counting system, based on the number 10. Apparently, someone in late Ubaidian times invented it, and early Sumerian thinkers adopted and refined it. The numbers in the system were represented by little clay tokens that a person could carry and use for calculating. Each stood for a single sheep, a measure of grain, or simply the number 1. A separate token signified 10 sheep, as well as the number 10. Thus, for instance, a person indicated the number 45 by displaying four number 10 tokens and five number 1 tokens.

When the Sumerians introduced the cuneiform writing system shortly before 3000 BC, there was no longer a need for people to carry around the physical tokens. Instead, scribes created wedge-shaped symbols equivalent to the numbers in the older system. By the late third millennium BC, there were two of these symbols—a vertical wedge and a corner wedge. These could have many different meanings depending on how one inscribed them on a tablet. Thus, if written one way, they might stand for 60 (6 x 10). Arranged another way, they might indicate 3,600 (60 x 60). Every number was a multiple of or divisible by either 6 or 10, making it a sort of sexagesimal scheme, a number system based on the number 60.

Thereafter, Mesopotamians continued to use the decimal system for numbers from 1 to 59. But larger numbers were indicated by a system that combined ideas from both the decimal and sexagesimal systems. By today's standards it was complicated and cumbersome, especially for larger numbers. If someone desired to indicate the number 11,437, for example, he wrote it as 3, 10, 37. Reading from right to left, the second number was an order of magnitude higher than the first, and the third an order higher than the second. People understood that the 3 stood for 3×60^2 (or 10,800), the 10 for 10 x 60 (or 600), and the 37 for 37 single decimal units. One then added the three numbers together: 10,800 + 600 + 37 = 11,437. Despite its complexity, a few components of this Babylonian system have survived, including counting 60 seconds to each minute, 60 minutes to each hour, and 360 degrees in a circle.

Doctors and Medicine

In addition to the first systematic celestial observations and counting systems, the ancient Mesopotamians produced some of the world's first doctors and medical advances. The oldest known surviving medical texts, on cuneiform tablets, were found in the ruins of the Sumerian cities, including Ur and Nippur. One dates to about 2300 BC, almost six centuries before the first known Egyptian medical writing.

Many of these texts describe very ancient folk beliefs that now appear odd and even ridiculous. One reads, "If he [the doctor] sees a black pig, that patient will die." A related one states that "if he sees a white pig, that patient will recover."[48] Similarly, many of the cures listed depended on magic, including chanting spells and charms over a patient or trying to drive out demons thought to be inhabiting the patient's body and thereby causing the illness. A doctor who took this magical, unscientific approach was called an *ashipu*.

There was, however, another kind of doctor, called an *asu*, who used more practical approaches to healing, such as giving patients herbal remedies. An *asu* had no more idea about what caused diseases and other medical conditions than an *ashipu* did. After all, the invention of the microscope and discovery of germs lay thousands of years in the future.

Yet some Mesopotamian doctors were no less observant than modern ones. So some of them noticed that a person could somehow catch certain illnesses from someone else, and therefore it was wise to keep a sick person from interacting with others. One of the surviving letters of Mari's king Zimri-Lim alludes to this astute medical observation. "I have heard that the lady Nanname has been taken ill," the letter begins. "She

Looking Back

The First Wagons and Carts

The widespread use of the wheel in Mesopotamia in Sumerian times made the invention of the first wagons in the region almost inevitable. The earliest wheels employed for these vehicles were made of solid wood, so they were very heavy. The late, noted historian Lionel Casson describes such wagons as having

> a box-like body borne on four solid wheels and drawn by teams either of oxen or onagers, a type of wild ass. Some remains dating back [to] about 2500 B.C. have been excavated, and these all belong to wagons that were quite small, the bodies only twenty inches or so broad and the wheels twenty to forty inches in diameter. This may have been the size that the onagers pulled, since any larger wagon of so massive a style would be too much for them. Indeed, pictures [paintings and sculpted reliefs] of the age more often than not show the beasts hitched in teams of four rather than just two. The two-wheeled cart seems to have made its debut slightly later than the wagon. It also was a massive affair fitted with solid wheels. Around 2300 B.C., the horse was introduced into the Middle East as a draught-animal, and within a few centuries a lighter type of cart, drawn by horses or mules, came into being, a fast and handy conveyance for kings, princes, high dignitaries, and the like.

Lionel Casson, *Travel in the Ancient World*. Baltimore, MD: Johns Hopkins University Press, 1994, p. 23.

has many contacts with the people of the palace. She meets many ladies in her house. Now then, give severe orders that no one should drink [from] the cup [from which] she drinks, no one should sit on the seat where she sits, no one should sleep in the bed where she sleeps [because] this disease is contagious."[49]

Knowing that disease existed and explaining it were two different things, however. Because they knew nothing of germs, Mesopotamian doctors tried to come up with other explanations. For instance, one assumption was that evil forces inhabiting one person's body could transfer into the body of a well person who came too close to the sick person.

Thus, the Mesopotamian medical profession had little in common with its modern counterpart. One exception is the symbol those ancient physicians employed to identify their profession. It consisted of a staff with snakes encircling it. Ancient Greek doctors later adopted the symbol, and modern doctors borrowed it from them, constituting still another of the many surviving elements of Mesopotamian culture in the modern world.

Building Innovations

While many medical treatments in the Tigris-Euphrates valley were based on superstition and were useless, another area of applied science and technology—monumental architecture—produced much more practical and useful results. In fact, advances in architecture and building methods made the early Mesopotamian urban centers possible. In these centers the world's first large-scale temples, palaces, and towering defensive walls arose.

For the most part these structures were made from the same materials as private houses—mud-bricks made from clay, which was abundant in the region. For the palaces and temples, however, the government-sponsored builders supplemented the bricks with some imported wooden timbers and big stone blocks. Also, for decorations they employed some expensive metals, including gold and silver.

In addition, where possible, builders used mortar to make the brick walls stronger and a bit more permanent. One kind of mortar was made from bitumen, a sticky, tar-like, petroleum-based substance. It came from isolated pools that formed on the ground here and there across the river valley. (The ancient residents did not realize that these pools were a minor residue from huge underground reservoirs of oil, which modern Iraq and many of its neighbors extract through drilling.)

Mesopotamian builders also employed two early technological advances for the tops of doors and passageways. One was the post-and-lintel. It consisted of a horizontal beam, the lintel, that sat atop two vertical supporting posts. One drawback was that if too much weight was stacked on top of the lintel, the beam could crack and the doorway could collapse. Trying to avoid this problem, where necessary the builders used an early Sumerian invention—the arch. It conveniently transferred the excess weight pressing down on the doorway outward and then downward into the ground. The builders also learned to erect a series of connected arches, forming the first vaulted tunnels, hallways, and chambers.

WORDS IN CONTEXT
bitumen
A tar-like, petroleum-based material used for mortar in building.

These materials and building methods were used for more than palaces, temples, and defensive walls. They were also applied to a distinctive monument unique to ancient Mesopotamia—the ziggurat. This was an enormous pyramid-like structure erected mainly in urban centers. Because ziggurats were used for religious purposes, they were almost always situated near temples.

At first glance a completed ziggurat looks a bit like an Egyptian pyramid, yet the two architectural forms are actually quite different. Egypt's pyramids were constructed as tombs for that nation's kings. In contrast, ziggurats were meant to be the central focus of ongoing religious worship. Another major difference is that the large Egyptian pyramids have inner chambers and passageways, whereas ziggurats are made of solid brick through and through.

Also, Egypt's pyramids are smooth and featureless on the outside. By comparison, a Mesopotamian ziggurat has a large stairway or ramp on which priests walked to reach a small chapel or temple on the building's summit. These special features of ziggurats reflect that they were intended as stairways to heaven. That is, priests and/or kings used the summit chapels as places for supposed private communication with the gods.

Travel and Transportation

Monumental ziggurats, temples, and palaces made the Mesopotamian cities marvels to behold in their heyday, the third and second millennia BC. In order for the residents of a city to impress visitors from other cities, those visitors had to engage in long-distance travel. That created a demand for improved means of transportation, still another area in which the people of the region pioneered technical innovations.

Before the advent of these advances, Mesopotamians relied on the most basic forms of transport, including walking, riding donkeys, and floating down the local rivers in small boats of rudimentary design. Typical of these vessels were canoes made from bundled river reeds and coracles, essentially round reed baskets coated with bitumen on the bottom to make them waterproof. There were also small wooden boats that moved upstream via attached ropes pulled by people walking along the nearby shore.

> **WORDS IN CONTEXT**
> **ziggurat**
> An enormous brick mound with a stairway leading up to a chapel on the top, used for religious purposes.

These early boats were not large, sturdy, and manageable enough to venture out into more turbulent open waterways like the Persian Gulf, Red Sea, and Indian Ocean. In about 3000 BC, however, some bright southern Mesopotamian shipbuilders found ways to build larger, more seaworthy vessels. These were capable of traveling much longer distances, which opened the way for travel to and trade with India and the northeastern coasts of Africa.

Land travel was also revolutionized in the region through the introduction and spread of one of the greatest of all technological inventions—the wheel. This happened in the period lasting from about 3500 to about 3000 BC and led to the creation of the first wagons and chariots. Initially, they were crude and slow, with large, solid wheels that made them heavy and difficult to pull and steer.

A major improvement occurred in the second millennium BC with another important innovation—techniques that allowed for bending strips of wood to make wheel rims. Now, wagon and chariot makers

The ruins of the ziggurat of Ur suggest a stairway leading to heaven. Ancient Mesopotamia's priests and kings walked these steps to reach a small chapel at the summit. There they could engage in private conversation with the gods.

could attach spokes connecting that rim to a hub in the wheel's center. The new wheel that resulted was far lighter, so such vehicles could move faster and maneuver more easily.

To make travel by wagon and chariot, as well as foot and donkey, easier and faster, the Mesopotamians built roads. These consisted mostly of hard-packed earth, sometimes topped by layers of gravel. Because they were firm, level, and free from obstacles, they were a major improvement over the uneven dirt paths that people had used in prior centuries. Traders, royal messengers, armies, and ordinary travelers could now go from one city to another in a day or two, compared to four, five, or more days in the past. Such roads connected Ur to Nippur, which were about 100 miles (161 km) apart, and Babylon to Larsa (120 miles, or 193 km, apart).

Because such travel still required stopping for at least one night, some local rulers built hostels—rest stops with places to sleep, have a meal, and buy supplies. Modern experts think these inn-like facilities were similar to later Greek and Roman versions—one- or two-story buildings roughly 70 feet (21 m) long and 40 feet (12 m) wide. In addition to bedchambers, kitchens, and dining areas, they featured roofed areas to protect wagons and chariots; spare wagon wheels and axles; and a stable for the donkeys, onagers (wild asses), and/or horses that pulled the vehicles.

Into the Realm of Memory

Over the centuries, a majority of Mesopotamian travelers who used these facilities were traders. Those hardy long-distance merchants braved long journeys to exotic foreign lands in order to bring back goods to better the lives of their countrymen. Yet in the fullness of time it was more often the case that Mesopotamia itself appeared compelling to the people of other lands. Increasingly, roads and travel led outsiders to enter and often to lay down roots in the great valley of the Tigris and Euphrates.

Unfortunately for the natives, many of those new arrivals were conquerors—Elamites, Hittites, Persians, Greeks, Romans, Parthians, and

Arabs, to name only a few. Mesopotamia's high culture, extensive system of cities, and vast farming estates repeatedly beckoned to and became easy prey for such outsiders. As a result, the Babylonians and Assyrians, the immediate heirs to the Sumerian cradle of civilization, were eventually overrun. Their once great nations and empires passed from the historical stage into the realm of memory.

As this happened, cities that had once been wonders of the world steadily shrank in size and importance. In Gwendolyn Leick's words, the mightiest of them all, Babylon, "became a provincial town with a dwindling population and deserted and derelict city quarters." Finally, when what was left of ancient Babylon "disappeared under drifts of sand," she adds, "the memory of the old Mesopotamian cities was thus bequeathed to a new age and a new civilization."[50]

Source Notes

Introduction: Lives Dependent on the Rivers

1. Gwendolyn Leick, *The Babylonians*. London: Routledge, 2003, pp. 6–7.
2. W.H. McNeill, *The Rise of the West: A History of the Human Community*. Chicago: University of Chicago Press, 1992, p. 46.
3. McNeill, *The Rise of the West*, p. 48.

Chapter One: City-States and Their Residents

4. McNeill, *The Rise of the West*, p. 49.
5. Quoted in Alexander Heidel, *A Babylonian Genesis*. Chicago: University of Chicago Press, 1951, p. 62.
6. Quoted in Heidel, *A Babylonian Genesis*, p. 62.
7. Stephen Bertman, *Handbook to Life in Ancient Mesopotamia*. New York: Facts On File, 2003, p. 191.
8. Gwendolyn Leick, *Mesopotamia: The Invention of the City*. New York: Penguin, 2001, p. xviii.
9. Karen R. Nemet-Nejat, *Daily Life in Ancient Mesopotamia*. Peabody, MA: Hendrickson, 2002, pp. 103–105.
10. Bertman, *Handbook to Life in Ancient Mesopotamia*, p. 248.
11. Quoted in L.W. King, trans., "Hammurabi's Code of Laws," Exploring Ancient World Culture, University of Evansville. http://eawc .evansville.edu.
12. Quoted in King, "Hammurabi's Code of Laws."
13. H.W.F. Saggs, *Civilization Before Greece and Rome*. New Haven, CT: Yale University Press, 1989, p. 58.
14. Quoted in A. Leo Oppenheim, trans., "Babylonian and Assyrian Historical Texts: Sargon of Agade," in J.B. Pritchard, ed., *Ancient Near Eastern Texts Relating to the Old Testament*. Princeton, NJ: Princeton University Press, 1955, p. 267.

15. Samuel N. Kramer, *Cradle of Civilization*. New York: Time-Life, 1978, p. 102.

Chapter Two: Home, Family, and Children

16. Bertman, *Handbook to Life in Ancient Mesopotamia*, pp. 275–76.
17. Leick, *The Babylonians*, p. 72.
18. Nemet-Nejat, *Daily Life in Ancient Mesopotamia*, p. 124.
19. Leick, *Mesopotamia*, p. 117.
20. Quoted in King, "Hammurabi's Code of Laws."
21. Quoted in King, "Hammurabi's Code of Laws."
22. Nemet-Nejat, *Daily Life in Ancient Mesopotamia*, p. 128.
23. Quoted in Fordham University, "Babylonian Proverbs from the Library of Ashurbanipal, ca. 1600 B.C.," *Ancient History Sourcebook*. www.fordham.edu.
24. Quoted in King, "Hammurabi's Code of Laws."
25. Quoted in Fordham University, "Proverbs from Kengir (Sumer), ca. 2000 B.C.," *Ancient History Sourcebook*. www.fordham.edu.

Chapter Three: Writing, Literature, and the Arts

26. Leick, *Mesopotamia*, p. 60
27. Quoted in Samuel N. Kramer, *The Sumerians: Their History, Culture, and Character*. Chicago: University of Chicago Press, 1971, pp. 246–48.
28. Quoted in Maximilian Strek, *Ashurbanipal, King of Assyria*, vol. 2. Leipzig: J.C. Hinrichs, 1916, pp. 252–53.
29. Bertman, *Handbook to Life in Ancient Mesopotamia*, p. 149.
30. Quoted in W.G. Lambert, ed. and trans., *Babylonian Wisdom Literature*, vol. 1. Oxford: Oxford University Press, 1960, p. 127.
31. A. Leo Oppenheim, *Ancient Mesopotamia: Portrait of a Dead Civilization*. Chicago: University of Chicago Press, 1977, p. 15.
32. Quoted in Lionel Casson, *Libraries in the Ancient World*. New Haven, CT: Yale University Press, 2001, p. 90.
33. Quoted in Fordham University, "Proverbs from Kengir (Sumer), ca. 2000 B.C."
34. Quoted in Fordham University, "Babylonian Proverbs from the Library of Ashurbanipal, ca. 1600 B.C."

35. Quoted in Thorkild Jacobson, *The Treasures of Darkness: A History of Mesopotamian Religion.* New Haven, CT: Yale University Press, 1978, pp. 87–89.

36. Chester G. Starr, *A History of the Ancient World.* New York: Oxford University Press, 1991, p. 135.

37. Seton Lloyd, *The Art of the Ancient Near East.* London: Thames and Hudson, 1965, p. 86.

38. Lloyd, *The Art of the Ancient Near East*, pp. 93, 96, 98.

Chapter Four: Gods and Religious Beliefs
39. Kramer, *Cradle of Civilization*, p. 160.

40. Kramer, *Cradle of Civilization*, pp. 99–100.

41. Quoted in Lambert, *Babylonian Wisdom Literature*, p. 127.

42. Bertman, *Handbook to Life in Ancient Mesopotamia*, p. 115.

43. Quoted in University of Oxford (UK) Faculty of Oriental Studies, "Enlil and Ninlil," *Electronic Text Corpus of Sumerian Literature.* http://etcsl.orinst.ox.ac.uk.

44. Leick, *The Babylonians*, p. 155.

45. Quoted in Stephanie Dalley, ed. and trans., *Myths from Mesopotamia.* New York: Oxford University Press, 2000, p. 173.

Chapter Five: Science, Technology, and Travel
46. Bertman, *Handbook to Life in Ancient Mesopotamia*, p. 170.

47. Quoted in Tamsyn Barton, *Ancient Astrology.* London: Routledge, 1994, pp. 16–17.

48. Quoted in Saggs, *Civilization Before Greece and Rome*, p. 257.

49. Quoted in Georges Roux, *Ancient Iraq.* New York: Penguin, 1993, p. 370.

50. Leick, *Mesopotamia*, p. 274.

For Further Research

Books

Joan Aruz et al., eds., *Cultures in Contact: From Mesopotamia to the Mediterranean in the Second Millennium B.C.* New York: Metropolitan Museum of Art, 2013.

Paul Kriwaczek, *Babylon: Mesopotamia and the Birth of Civilization*. New York: Thomas Dunne, 2012.

Allison Lassieur, *Ancient Mesopotamia*. New York: Children's Press, 2012.

Gwendolyn Leick, *The A to Z of Mesopotamia*. New York: Scarecrow, 2010.

Christine Mayfield and Kristine M. Quinn, *Mesopotamia: World Cultures Through Time*. Westminster, CA: Teacher Created Materials, 2008.

James B. Pritchard, ed., *The Ancient Near East: An Anthology of Texts and Pictures*. Princeton, NJ: Princeton University Press, 2011.

Martha E.H. Rustad, *The Babylonians: Life in Ancient Babylon*. Minneapolis: Millbrook, 2009.

Websites

Ancient Mesopotamia: Archaeology (http://oi.uchicago.edu/OI/MUS/ED/TRC/MESO/archaeology.html). This site, run by the famed Oriental Institute of the University of Chicago, has several links to brief but informative articles about ancient Mesopotamia.

Assyria: A General Introduction (www.livius.org/as-at/assyria/assyria.html). A valuable overview of this important ancient Mesopotamian people.

A Collection of Contracts from Mesopotamia (www.fordham.edu /Halsall/ancient/mesopotamia-contracts.asp). Fordham University's *Ancient History Sourcebook* provides this revealing collection of ancient Mesopotamian contracts relating to marriage, divorce, adoption, loans, inheritances, and more.

Enuma Elish (www.sacred-texts.com/ane/enuma.htm). L.W. King's translation of the famous Babylonian creation epic.

Hammurabi (www.humanistictexts.org/hammurabi.htm). Contains excellent translations of many of that famous Babylonian ruler's laws.

Lamassu (www.livius.org/la-ld/lamassu/lamassu.html). A brief but useful description of the giant human-headed bull statues that guarded the entrances to Assyrian palaces.

Sumerian Mythology (http://home.comcast.net/~chris.s/sumer-faq .html). Christopher Siren's well-written introduction to the primary figures and tales of the early Mesopotamian myths.

Ziggurat (www.livius.org/za-zn/ziggurat/ziggurat.html). An excellent overview of the huge ancient Mesopotamian religious structures called ziggurats.

Index

Note: Boldface page numbers indicate illustrations.

rubbish, 21

sacred texts, 49
Saggs, H.W.F., 25
sanitary conditions, 21, 33
Sargon, 27–28
science
  agricultural, 17, 18, 19
  architectural, 16, 80–82, **83**
  as basis for early Greek science, 71
  mathematical, 77–78
  medical, 78, 80
  and sky observations, 71, 72–74, **73**
  transportation, 71–72, 79, 82–84
scribes, 44–47, 51
sculpture/sculptors, 53–54
serfs, 25–26
shade-tree gardening, 17
Shamash (Babylonian god), 49, 50
sheep, 19
Shulgi (Sumerian king), 75
Sin (Babylonian god), 60
sky observers/observations, 71, 72–74, **73**
slaves, 23–25, 32
  private, 24
  public, 23–24
Smith, George, 52
Starr, Chester G., 54
Sumerians
  agriculture of, 16–19
  architecture of, 81
  art of, **55**, 55–56
  astronomy of, 71
  cities of, 15–16
  clothing of, 34
  conquest of, 27, 50–51
  continuation of culture of, 28
  epic poetry of, 48
  mathematics of, 77
  proverbs of, 50
  roads of, 75
  writing developed by, 43
  See also city-states
superstition, 41

Tablet of Destiny, 64
technology
  agricultural, 17, 18, 19
  architectural, 16, 80–82, **83**
  road, 75, 84
  transportation, 71–72, 79, 82–84
teenagers, jobs of, 19
Tell al-Ubaid, 14
Tell al-Warka, 19
temperatures, 17
temples
  creation of cities by Marduk for, 15
  farming estates of, 19

first versions of, 14
in urban layout, 19
Tepe Gawra, 14
thatch, defined, 11
Tigris-Euphrates valley, 10–11, 13, **13**
Tigris River, 10–11, 13, **13**
time divisions, 76
townhouses, 30–31
toys, 41
trade and transportation, 82, 84
transportation, 71–72, 79, 82–84
tupsharru, 44

Ubaidians, 14–15, 58, 77
upper classes, 26–27
  fashion accessories of, 34
  food eaten by, 34, 36
  houses of, 33
Ur
  destruction of, 50–51
  population of, 14, 16
  status of noble women in, 38
  territory of, 27
Uruk
  layout of, 23
  population of, 14, 23
  ruins of, 19–20, **31**
  territory of, 27
Utu (Sumerian god), 46–47, 49, 50

Venus tablets, 74
villages, 10, 11, 14

wagons, 79, 82–83
wardu, 23–25
weaving, **25**
wheel, development of, 79, 82–83
wisdom literature, 50
women
  clothing and accessories of, 34, **37**
  makeup kits of, 34
  marriage of slaves to free-born, 32
  noble, 38
  occupations of, 38
  in patriarchal society, 36–38
  position of Assyrian, 35
  scribes, 46–47
  status of noble, in Ur, 38
  weaving, **25**
Wood, Michael, 23
Woolley, Charles Leonard, 18
writing, **45**
  development of, 43–44
  mathematics and, 77
  medical text, 78
  scribes for, 44–46, 51

ziggurats, 81–82, **83**

Picture Credits

About the Author

Historian and award-winning author Don Nardo has written numerous books about the ancient world, its peoples, and their cultures, including volumes on the Babylonians, Assyrians, Persians, Minoans, Greeks, Etruscans, Romans, and others. He is also the author of single-volume encyclopedias on ancient Mesopotamia, ancient Greece, ancient Rome, and Greek and Roman mythology. Nardo, who also composes and arranges orchestral music, lives with his wife, Christine, in Massachusetts.